GUITAR
T A B
EDITION

Etudes *for* Electric Guitar
Book 1

Twelve solo pieces for guitar
in standard notation and tab by Kris Lennox.

T0039709

Published by
WISE PUBLICATIONS
14-15 Berners Street, London W1T 3LJ, UK.

Exclusive Distributors:
MUSIC SALES LIMITED
Distribution Centre, Newmarket Road,
Bury St Edmunds, Suffolk IP33 3YB, UK.

MUSIC SALES CORPORATION
180 Madison Avenue, 24th Floor,
New York, NY 10016, USA.

MUSIC SALES PTY LIMITED
4th floor, Lisgar House, 30-32 Carrington Street,
Sydney, NSW 2000, Australia.

Order No. AM1010922
ISBN: 978-1-78305-954-6
This book © Copyright 2015 Wise Publications,
a division of Music Sales Limited.

Unauthorised reproduction of any part of this
publication by any means including photocopying
is an infringement of copyright.

Edited by Adrian Hopkins.
Guitar recorded by Kris Lennox.
Mixed and mastered by Jonas Persson.
Cover design by Tim Field.
Printed in the EU.

Etudes *for* Electric Guitar
Book 1

Twelve solo pieces for guitar
in standard notation and tab by Kris Lennox.

WISE PUBLICATIONS
part of The Music Sales Group
London / New York / Paris / Sydney / Copenhagen /
Berlin / Madrid / Hong Kong / Tokyo

YOUR GUARANTEE OF QUALITY:

As publishers, we strive to produce every
book to the highest commercial standards.

This book has been carefully designed
to minimise awkward page turns and
to make playing from it a real pleasure.

Particular care has been given to specifying
acid-free, neutral-sized paper made from pulps
which have not been elemental chlorine bleached.

This pulp is from farmed sustainable forests and
was produced with special regard for the environment.

Throughout, the printing and binding have been
planned to ensure a sturdy, attractive publication
which should give years of enjoyment.

If your copy fails to meet our high standards,
please inform us and we will gladly replace it.

www.musicsales.com

INTRODUCTION

The electric guitar is one of the most versatile instruments. It is constantly evolving, with many new innovations – e.g., effects pedals, locking tremolo systems, number of strings, tuning system etc.

Given the versatility (and popularity) of electric guitar, it is very surprising that it lacks a developed solo repertoire. Yes, there are many *solos* for electric guitar – but how many *solo works?* How many solo works can you think of? 20? 10? 5? 2?

Why is this? Why does the electric guitar lack a solo repertoire? I've considered this for almost as long as I've played guitar. I believe there are a number of reasons, the primary ones being:

1) When we learn electric guitar, we generally learn parts from songs. We learn the rhythm part, we learn the lead part – but what we learn is always a single thread from a far bigger tapestry. Ingrained in our thinking is the idea that the electric guitar is an ensemble instrument – it is part of a band setup. Over many years, it becomes very difficult to see the electric guitar as anything else.

2) Most electric guitarists we know and love are busy touring – they simply don't have time to score their music, or to develop solo material.

3) (Take note that this is an observation and not a criticism) Most electric guitarists can't read music. This has its pros and cons, but one of the biggest drawbacks is that electric guitarists rarely score their music – simply because they can't. In the majority of instances, the closest we get to playing works by the guitarists we love is by watching them play (then copying), or buying TAB books with transcribed parts.

4) Writing a solo work requires an entirely different approach, compositionally. When writing as part of a band, we have all other instruments to imply chords etc. – we can do far less, yet the music will sound cohesive: one note can sound fantastic in a band context – one note in a solo work has a very different effect. The solo work has to imply harmony in and of itself: everything changes.

What could help electric guitar in respect to the above is a formalised repertoire. If you meet a pianist who can play all of Chopin's *Etudes,* it is guaranteed they could play almost everything written for piano (Chopin's *Etudes* cover almost every conceivable technical difficulty at the piano). The same could be said of the violinist who can play all of Paganini's *Caprices.*

With guitar, we have no way of discerning the level of each player. If I can play Satriani's *Flying in a Blue Dream,* do I have the technical ability to play Slipknot's 'The Blister Exists'? Or Periphery's 'Zyglrox'? Or anything at all by Tosin Abasi? It all becomes very grey.

Initially required in the creation of a solo electric guitar repertoire are works that highlight the technical difficulties of playing – works that, if the player could play all of them, would guarantee a technical grounding that covers all (presently) possible/knowable difficulties on the instrument. Works that, if mastered, would guarantee the player a technical level capable of playing almost anything put in front of them. The logical method of approaching this would be creating volumes of *Etudes* (*Etude* simply means *Study*: a work focusing on specific technical aspect/aspects of playing).

Of course, such difficulties can be found in the music around us: the difference with an etude is that a specific technical difficulty is exaggerated and given focus to the point where the performer *has* to overcome the difficulty, or they simply won't be able to perform the work. One of our favourite tunes may have a burst of hammer-ons/pull-offs that we struggle with and simply overlook. This is impossible with a work that consists of nothing *but* hammer-ons/pull-offs. Exposing technique in such a way can either inspire or terrify!

DO I NEED A SPECIAL TYPE OF ELECTRIC GUITAR?

All works in this book (and all forthcoming *Etudes* books) are written with certain constraints in mind. The constraints are as follows:

1) No work will go beyond the 21st fret

2) No locking tremolo arm is required

3) No effects pedals are required

4) Only 6 strings are required

5) Apart from distortion, no effects are required – however, the works can be played clean if desired

The primary reason for the above constraints is to create works approachable/accessible to all electric guitarists, from the most advanced guitarist to the guitarist who only recently purchased their first electric guitar/amp combo from the local supermarket.

If works were composed that spanned to the 24th fret, a more specialised guitar would be required – which would place the works out of reach of a large chunk of the electric guitar playing population. The same could be said with regards all other constraints outlined above.

In following the above constraints, there is only one thing holding the guitarist back from being able to play these works: dedication.

There is certainly a place for solo works focusing on 7/8/9 string guitars, guitars with locking trems, works with delay pedal etc. – I personally hope such works are created – and I intend to create solo repertoire in these fields in the future.

However, if I were to create such works as part of these *Etudes,* it would contradict the original intention of composing sets of studies which open the world of solo electric guitar playing to everyone who owns an electric guitar, and not only those with more specialised equipment.

HOW SHOULD I USE THIS BOOK?

You can use this book in any manner you wish. It all depends on what you hope to achieve. There are no rules.

You could, for example, use this book as a resource of useful and interesting arpeggio shapes to add to your own soloing. This is ok! (As a matter of fact, prior to this book being released, one of my guitar-playing friends worked through one of the *Etudes*. He didn't actually learn it as a piece of music, but took some of the ideas from it and added them to his own playing. He demonstrated by improvising a solo which included a number of the arpeggio shapes he learned. And it sounded *fantastic*.)

You could also use the book as a good study tool for rhythmic groupings. You could, for example, use one of the rhythmic groupings used in one of the *Etudes* as the rhythmic basis for one of your own compositions.

Here are a few other ideas:

- You could analyse the chord progressions and use some of the changes in your own pieces

- You could study the fingering

- You could look at how the pieces use open strings to move efficiently and smoothly up/down the neck

Again, how you use the book is limited only by your own imagination.

In saying this, the works do serve a definite purpose, which is, of course, the development of alternate picking/cross-picking technique. If you hope to maximise your skills in this respect, I'd suggest following the performance instructions exactly as they are written: doing so will facilitate maximum performance gains.

Performance instructions shouldn't be seen as limiting, but as tools which allow you to achieve 'maximum potential'.

WHY NO NAMES FOR THE WORKS?

Composers are often asked why many of their pieces have no titles and are simply named according to the musical material. You'll more often find a composer calling a piece 'Study in F♯m' than 'The Magical Bacon Potato'.

It is often assumed that composers give their works 'dry titles' from lack of imagination. In some instances this may well be true. However, there are a number of reasons 'dry' titles can be preferable. I'll give what are, for me, the two main reasons why a 'dry' title could, in certain instances, be preferable. The first reason is practical, the second aesthetic.

1) 'Dry' titles give the performer an idea of what *kind* of work the musical work is. This can be seen as advantageous or disadvantageous, depending on perspective. It can be disadvantageous in the sense that it can make certain aspects of the piece predictable before the piece is even heard. However, it can be advantageous in the sense that if, for example, you're looking for a technically involving piece of music, you'll know that a work titled *Etude* will give you what you want. You don't have to trawl the history of written/recorded music looking for something appropriate – your search can be far more specific.

If a composer is writing a work for a musician, a 'dry' title is possibly preferable, as it acts like a roadmap. If a work is written for the layperson (i.e. *not* a trained musician), a creative title is possibly preferable. In this sense, the intended market could be seen as having significance with respect to the title of the work.

2) Creative titles can, ironically, narrow possibility and limit the performer/listener's imaginative potential. If I told you *Etude in D* was to be titled 'Florida Sunshine Study' (I'm making an example here – it *wasn't* going to be called that!), to a point I'm funnelling your thoughts into what could be seen as a narrow alleyway.

The more information I give you as to what I imagine a piece to be, the less room there is for you to impress yourself upon it. What is created is an instance where you could say to your friend, with respect to a certain piece, something along the lines of "To me this passage sounds like falling rain", and your friend could reply "That's just wrong, as the title of the piece is 'Desert Heat'". If your vision (or the composer's) clashes with my vision, it can cause unrest (I've had this myself with a number of pieces. With one work in particular, I simply couldn't hear what the composer said the work was meant to sound like. Part of me felt inadequate as a consequence of this. Again, there are a number of ways of looking at this: my creative imagination was inadequate, or the composer's execution of his vision was poor – or the performer gave a bad performance).

If a composer/songwriter has a specific vision, their piece will probably have a specific title with respect to this vision – but not having a specific title doesn't necessarily mean a work has no vision as such.

With these *Etudes,* there are no creative titles for the sake of giving the performer (and listener) imaginative freedom. If you hear a passage in your mind as sounding like bells, this is great. No one can tell you this is wrong: your mind is your mind (conversely, it would be unfair of you to tell someone else that their view is 'wrong' as it is different from your own view).

Creatively, it is very important to *never* lose the integrity of your own thoughts.

INTERPRETATION

Interpretation is the art of *deciding how to play a composition*. This concept is relatively alien to exclusively electric guitarists, where the main aim in learning a solo is often *Imitation* and not *Interpretation*.

When growing up, I wanted to play my favourite solos *exactly* as they sounded on the recording. This meant an obsessive attention to detail/nuance. My aim was to perform over a backing track and my own solo to be an exact blueprint of the original. I'd spend entire school holidays taking this approach with tracks such as Steve Vai's 'The Riddle'.

I remember hearing Vai perform 'The Riddle' live, and I was left feeling disappointed. 'But he changed parts of it!' I thought to myself. For me, the perfection of the track was the audio recording. Altering any part of it was, in my mind, sacrilege – even if the creator himself was the one altering (note: I was 14 at the time).

After studying improvisation for a number of years, I slowly began to realise that in many instances the guitarist will, to put it crudely, simply be playing with ideas over a backing track. The appeal of improvisation is, of course, controlled freedom. When I started composing my own guitar works, I realised that a certain passage would have an *Intention* (i.e. in one passage I'd be trying to convey, for example, anger), and the project was to *create the intention more than creating a blueprint*. This was freeing, in the sense that it opened up a new mode of perception for me: I could now listen to my favourite musicians perform and appreciate the creative changes they made rather than seeing such changes as a negative.

Many non-Classical musicians dismiss Classical music for its apparent lack of freedom. Yes, the score is fixed, but the freedom lies in the *Interpretation*. For example: how loud is loud? Your loud may be louder than my loud. How much have I to slow down when I've to slow down? Have I to park the car in the drive, or just drop the speed a little?

Again, controlled freedom.

The Rock approach, which primarily consists of improvisation, is very different from the Classical approach (where there is (with the exception of a handful of pieces) no freedom with respect to notes used). Both approaches have their advantages and drawbacks. A study of both is certainly an advantage when it comes to composition/general musical creativity.

Many Rock musicians, when handed a musical score, don't know where to start, as they can't read. Many Classical musicians, when handed a chord sheet and asked to improvise, don't know where to start, as their entire musical life has consisted of reading and not improvising. There is no right or wrong – there are simply approaches that work better in certain situations.

I remember one of my most enlightening piano lessons as a youngster. I was working on Liszt's 'Ballade No. 2', and took the score to one of my piano teachers. I was about 5 minutes in to performing the work, when my teacher stopped me and gave me a list of every recording I had listened to of the piece.

How did she know which recordings I had? Simple – I was interpreting the score in certain ways that wasn't an *interpretation,* but a copy of how other pianists had played certain sections. I still wasn't bringing my own ideas to the music.

She asked me questions such as 'Are you speeding up in this section because you feel the music should get faster, or are you simply copying pianist x's recording?' I was stumped – and she knew I was copying. Many Classical performers adopt this approach – but they'll widen their reach and listen to tens of recordings and borrow ideas from each recording. To reach a truly individual voice takes years – and requires a high degree of self-confidence.

A long time ago I abandoned listening to recordings of works I intended to perform. Some works I still don't touch, as burnt into my mind are certain performances of the works that I hold to be 'ideal'. deal'. I cannot forget certain recordings – my own interpretations will, as a result of this, lack 'purity'.

With these *Etudes,* it is very important to me that the guitarist bring something of their own personality to their performances. You'll notice my recordings are very 'straight' (i.e. almost metronomic, no real variation in dynamics etc.) – this is intentional, and for a number of reasons.

If I were to, for example, slow down in a certain passage, there's a good chance that everyone would also slow down in that passage. I'd rather the performer slowed down as they thought the music sounded like it *ought* to slow down, and not because they heard the recording where *I* slowed down. Again, it's the difference between interpretation and imitation.

The notes/fingering/picking of the *Etudes* is fixed. However, I encourage *complete freedom with interpretation.* If you think a passage would sound good entirely palm-muted, by all means palm-mute the entire section. If you think a certain note should have vibrato, add vibrato. If you think a passage would sound more dramatic if you played it faster, play it faster! I'm keeping the 'canvas of interpretation' blank as I want to encourage the performer to trust their vision of the music. Your vision is not 'wrong', as I'm not specifying exactly what you should do with the music.

What I'd discourage is listening to how other people play the pieces and copying their ideas. If you don't have your own ideas, sit the music down and come back to it when you feel you have something to say with it.

In saying this, beware of a common compensation many musicians make which they then describe as 'interpretation': speeding up when a passage is easy, and slowing down when a passage is difficult. I used to lie to myself with certain passages by saying 'But it sounds good slower' – the truth is, I knew it was too difficult for me to play at speed. I was slowing down to compensate for my own technical inadequacy. In musical terms, we would call this *Tempo Compensation.*

In most instances, great performers will speed up at busy passages (it adds to the drama), and if anything, they'll slow down at the 'easy' passages (it often adds to the lyricism).

I'd personally recommend playing the works from start to finish with the metronome before focusing on interpretation. This should 'iron out' technical problems such as potential tempo compensation.

Consider my recordings as tools to let you hear the music (i.e. the progressions/overall sound etc.), but not a guide as to how the works should be interpreted. Try to make a distinction in your mind between a *technical performance* (i.e. playing strictly in time with the metronome – which will take your technique very far indeed), and a *musical interpretation.*

Also, don't feel inadequate if you have no ideas of your own with regards how to interpret a work – you can still use each work as a tool to vastly improve technique.

MOTO PERPETUO

Moto Perpetuo simply means *perpetual motion*. Constant notes, if you will.

Every piece in this book is written in the *moto perpetuo* manner. There are no breaks in rhythm from the beginning of each work until the very end.

The works are written in this manner for a number of reasons:

1) **Stamina.** Playing constantly with no rest requires considerable stamina – especially so in the right hand, given every note of these *Etudes* is picked.

2) **Ease of reading.** Many electric players don't read rhythm – they often copy how a piece sounds rather than understanding how notes fall against a beat. No change in rhythm means you don't have to worry about the rhythm: all you have to do is switch on the metronome and play evenly.

3) **Accuracy of timing.** With constant notes, a 'slip of rhythm' is very obvious to the ear. If one of your notes is slightly early/late, it'll stand out more than an early/late note in a piece where the rhythm changes often. Timing/evenness of playing is greatly improved in moto perpetuo works.

(In forthcoming *Electric Etudes* books, only certain pieces are composed in the moto perpetuo style. Many pieces have rhythms that frequently change. For players considering working through future editions of the *Etudes*, I would recommend a study of rhythm.)

TAB is a fantastic way of learning music on guitar. It is very natural to read, and is a far more accessible way of 'getting at the music' than learning to read standard notation – which can take years to read well (learning to read standard notation fluently can take as long as it takes to learn to *read* fluently).

In saying this, TAB is not without its drawbacks. One of the downsides of reading TAB is lack of rhythmic notation. Studying musical rhythm/practising drumming exercises etc. is of great importance to the guitarist.

Rhythm is one of the primary elements of music (alongside pitch, dynamics, silence etc.): to overlook rhythm is equivalent to building a house with no outer walls.

After a study of rhythm, you'll probably find relying on audio as an illustration of how something should be played will no longer be necessary. You'll be able to look at the musical notation **and** the TAB, and combine information from both. You'll be able to look at the notated music and discern how the notes should fall against the beat (i.e. the rhythm). Using musical notation for rhythm is far easier than the rhythmic notation frequently used as part of the TAB system.

TEMPO

The pieces in this book don't have a fixed tempo. Guitarists will be aware of how odd this is. When composers write a piece, they normally have a fixed idea of the piece in their mind – which translates to a fixed tempo for the piece.

With an etude, having a fixed tempo could actually be seen as a limiting factor. Let's assume I specify a work is to be played at, for example, 120BPM. A fixed tempo indirectly creates three categories of performers:

- Those who find the indicated tempo too fast

- Those who can play the work at the indicated tempo

- Those who find the indicated tempo too slow

Ironically, all three categories of player will have less motivation to practise a work than if it *didn't* have a fixed tempo:

- If you struggle to play a work at the indicated tempo, there's a good chance the sense of inadequacy due to the struggle will result in lack of desire to practise the work

- If you can play a work at the indicated tempo, why bother practising it?

- The ability to play faster than the indicated tempo would suggest there really isn't much of a technical challenge to be found in the work.

All *Etudes* have a **suggested minimum tempo,** rather than a fixed tempo.

You may be able to play the works far faster than I could ever play them. For me to say of each work 'this work becomes difficult at a tempo of…' would be relatively short-sighted.

(A sprint athlete could probably jog 100m faster than you or I could sprint 100m. For the sprint athlete, the speed you and I sprint at would probably be slower than their warm-up speed.)

Conversely, you may find the tempi I've performed these works at ridiculously fast. The tempi of my recordings are the tempi I feel I can play the works at smoothly, and with full physical and mental control; nothing more, nothing less. My recorded tempi aren't the 'correct' tempi.

There is no 'correct' tempo for each piece.

For many players, the suggested minimum tempo of each piece will feel very fast. To begin with, dismiss tempo entirely, and focus on playing with accuracy and clarity. Working the tempo should be a secondary issue.

(I'd suggest *always* using the metronome when practising; it'll 'iron out' any technical difficulties you're having. Stay slow and stay even – use the metronome as a tool to improve evenness prior to using it as a tool for gaining speed. To begin with, consider the metronome a *rhythm monitor* rather than an *accelerometer*.)

For some players, simply playing through a work and keeping in time – even very slowly – will be challenge enough.

Your playing will develop more by playing through these works at a very slow speed than not playing the works at all. Being able to play a work at, for example, one note a beat at 60BPM is still playing the work (note also that playing slowly and with clarity will be far better for your technique than playing fast and sloppy). The tempo is irrelevant, and progress will be made in due course anyway. If you increased the metronome by 1BPM every second day, you'd be over 180BPM faster within a year.

The *suggested minimum tempo* of each piece is the tempo that requires 'good' technique in order to maintain the tempo. This isn't simply a matter of my own personal opinion: I've given the *Etudes* to other guitarists, and my suggested minimum tempi are the tempi at which, in general, guitarists begin to find the works difficult. If you can play all 12 *Etudes* at the suggested minimum tempi – and with proper technique/execution – you will have reached a secure level of proficiency with respect to the techniques outlined in this book.

The suggested minimum tempo for each work is simply that: a *suggestion*. Don't be put off if a tempo is beyond you – and don't hold back if the tempo is beneath you.

There is no upper limit to the tempo of each piece. This is where things have the potential to become *very interesting indeed*.

Some guitarists can play very, *very* fast. For such guitarists, they'll have to play far faster than a slower guitarist to reap similar technical gains, as their own technical ability will have reached such a level that what may, for you and me, be very fast playing indeed, is nothing more than a jog for them. Fast players will really have to push the tempo to challenge themselves.

A truly competitive element could arise as a consequence of the open nature of the tempi: we may find an instance where a guitarist posts a recording of a work online at, for example, 140BPM, only to be superseded the following week by another guitarist playing the same work at 142BPM.

This doesn't mean the 'aim of the game' is to play every work as fast as possible: you may like the sound of a certain work at a certain tempo – this approach is to be applauded: a musical interpretation will have more impact than a purely technical demonstration. There is space for both approaches. Both are to be encouraged.

My personal advice is to be extra-vigilant of how clean your performances are. It is easy to play fast and messy – most guitarists could play fast and messy. The aim is to play fast *and* with clarity.

If you are going to be 'in competition' with someone, it is best to be in competition with *yourself,* and only yourself. Set goals to go beyond your *own* limits. Set tempo goals. Set goals to play as clean as possible. Set goals to play as musically as possible. Set goals to play as evenly as possible etc.

Ultimately, the validity of recordings/performances will be decided by the guitar-playing community as a whole. Great technical *and* musical performances will, I'm sure, be admired by all. First and foremost, play for *yourself*, and not for praise. The journey is the reward.

RHYTHMIC GROUPINGS

If we played constant semiquavers in 4/4 time, we'd have 16 semiquavers per bar (hence in the US semiquavers are known as *16th notes*).

We normally group semiquavers per beat: in 4/4, this would give us 4 semiquavers per beat.

There are many ways of counting semiquavers – some common ways are outlined below:

1 2 3 4 **1** 2 3 4 **1** 2 3 4 **1** 2 3 4

1 2 3 4 **2** 2 3 4 **3** 2 3 4 **4** 2 3 4

1 e & a **2** e & a **3** e & a **4** e & a

Co-ca co-la **Co**-ca co-la **Co**-ca co-la **Co**-ca co-la etc.

We can make our music far more interesting by abandoning the notion of groups of 4, and creating our own groupings. If our new groupings total 16, they will work in 4/4 time. For example – I could create a grouping of 3-4-3-4-2 – which will work in 4/4, as the groupings add up to 16.

I could count this as follows:

1 2 3 **1** 2 3 4 **1** 2 3 **1** 2 3 4 **1** 2

This is a very interesting pattern which changes the feel of 4/4, as the natural groupings of 4 have been broken. 4/4 can, for musicians, at times feel 'mundane' when the semiquavers are grouped in 4's, as the musician's ear has come to expect groupings of 4. In one sense, the music has become predictable. Many Mathcore bands create unusual groupings of semiquavers to give their music an unpredictable feel. It is a great effect – and the principle is one worth keeping in your 'composition toolbox'. **Odd rhythmic groupings can be used to create interest and give a sense of unpredictability.**

A number of works in this book use odd rhythmic groupings. One of the most unusual is *Etude in Cm*, which groups the semiquavers as 2-2-3-4-5.

You could count these groupings as follows:

1 2 **1** 2 **1** 2 3 **1** 2 3 4 **1** 2 3 4 5

Rhythmic groupings are indicated in the introductory text for each work.

ARPEGGIOS

In terms of pitches, a melody consists of, by definition, two units: scales and arpeggios. If we have one alphabet letter after another (i.e C-D), we have part of a scale. If we have any type of jump (i.e C-E, C-F etc.), we have part of an arpeggio. All we have when creating a single-note melody are steps or skips. Nothing else is possible (with the exception of repeats (e.g C-C on the same pitch), which can be classed as part of a scale *or* an arpeggio; whether it is classed as a scale or arpeggio is determined, in each instance, by musical context).

Scales/arpeggios have always been the building blocks for melodies. They are, primarily, compositional tools. This may sound strange to any classical player who has grown up with the grade system, or any player who hasn't studied composition: to such players, scales and arpeggios are viewed as a means of acquiring technique.

Of course, scales/arpeggios are great for acquiring technique, but if they are viewed *solely* as a means of acquiring technique, only one aspect of their useful function is being harnessed. It is always good practice to have more than one reason for pursuing something; if you only have one reason for doing something, your motivation to pursue it will fade/vanish when the reason becomes irrelevant.

This is very apparent with musicians: if you play guitar solely for enjoyment, you'll play it far less than the person who plays for enjoyment *and* the development of, for example, self-discipline. Let's assume you play solely for enjoyment: if you wake up one day and have no desire to practise, you won't practise. If you play for enjoyment *and* discipline, and wake up one day with no desire to practise, you can view this as an opportunity to use guitar practise as a means of developing self-discipline ('not enjoying it' doesn't matter in this instance, as you have more reasons for playing than enjoyment). I've had days where there was absolutely no enjoyment in my practise (I'm sure we've all had this!) – on such days though, it didn't matter to me that I wasn't 'enjoying myself', as I had other reasons for practising aside from enjoyment (playing an instrument can be about far more than enjoyment – it is good to keep this in mind when motivation is low. Of course we enjoy playing – but there's far more to it than *just enjoyment*. The pressure to be enjoying every moment of what we do can be quite a distraction).

The same is true of any tool – if you're tired of practising scales/arpeggios as a means of developing technique, you could try using them to develop your musical/compositional vocabulary (and vice versa).

I'm often surprised when speaking to classical players when I ask them what an arpeggio is. The answer given 99% of the time is 'the notes of a chord played in order one after another' – which is partially true, and partially false. If an instrument is nearby and I ask them to demonstrate, they'll play an arpeggio in the manner of what is required for an exam, i.e. the C major arpeggio would be played C-E-G.

A more accurate definition of an arpeggio would be **the notes of a chord played one at a time.** And to compensate for the common misconception of an arpeggio as the notes of a chord played in sequence, we could define an arpeggio as **the notes of a chord played one at a time, in any order.** The sequence of the notes is irrelevant to the satisfying of the conditions of the definition.

If we take a C major chord, we have the notes C-E-G. Imagine we have these notes as letters on bingo balls, and they are in a bag. We have the 'C major bag'. If we were to pick these balls from the bag, the result would always be a C major chord, irrespective of order. C-E-G = C major, E-C-G = C major etc. etc.

The same is also true if we add more of the same notes. We could add five G's, three E's, and two C's to our bag, and we'd still have the 'C major bag'. If we picked out G-G-E-C-E-C-C-G, we'd *still* have a C major arpeggio. We haven't added any new alphabet letters to our bag (which would change the chord) – we've simply added more of the same letters.

This is also true when playing arpeggios on an instrument. We could play a 'pure' C major arpeggio on the guitar (i.e C-E-G), or we could change the order (i.e E-C-G), or increase the quantity of each note (i.e C-C-G-E-E-G): all are C major arpeggios.

Take note also that the pitches can be on any octave – we can have C's on different octaves, and it doesn't change the *quality* of the chord (i.e it doesn't change it from major to minor).

In music, we call the arrangement of the notes of an arpeggio/chord the *voicings*. C-E-G = one voicing, E-G-C = another voicing. We can have one arpeggio, but many *voicings* of each arpeggio.

This becomes more obvious on instruments with a wider range than the guitar (e.g. the piano), where there are many ways to play chords/arpeggios (i.e there are a great number of voicings). Orchestral composers often expand on this and create voicings that are impossible to play on single instruments (voicings that would require a stretch beyond what the hands are capable of playing at any one instrument).

I have chosen arpeggios as the basic musical structure in this volume of *Etudes* for a number of reasons, the primary reasons being:

- Arpeggios imply chord progressions when there is no harmony, creating a fuller sound with a sense of harmonic movement, despite the presence of only one musical line

- Arpeggios naturally fall across the guitar strings as opposed to falling on a single string, very often creating picking difficulties (i.e. the technical aim of this volume)

- Many arpeggio shapes give rise to very odd/unusual left hand fingerings, developing LH technique

- Lead guitarists primarily think in a scalar manner: in this book, thinking in such a way is impossible due to the focus on arpeggios (with the result being new modes of thought at the instrument i.e. expanded creative possibilities)

- The arpeggio shapes in these *Etudes* can be learned by the player independent of each study and used as 'solo fragment' ideas (all shapes that don't incorporate open strings can be transposed into any key)

Note that on the musical score, no arpeggio names have been given (e.g. it *doesn't* say Am above an Am arpeggio, Fm7♭5 above an Fm7♭5 arpeggio etc.) – despite the strict *technical* focus of the *Etudes,* I want the player *musically* to feel a sense of discovery. You'll probably use certain arpeggios more in your own playing when you *discover* what they are, rather than when you are *told* what they are.

KEY SIGNATURE

Each piece in this book is written in a different key. If you aren't familiar with the notion of keys, you'd be forgiven for thinking a mistake has been made in stating each work is in a different key.

For example, there are two works in D (*Etude in D,* and *Etude in Dm)*, two works in E, etc.

Let's look at the D major and D minor scales:

D major = D E F♯ G A B C♯ D

D minor = D E F G A B♭ C D

They use a different set of notes.

The D minor scale is actually the F major scale (F major scale = F G A B♭ C D E F), but with a different starting point:

D minor = D E F G A B♭ C D

F major = F G A B♭ C D E F

(Both scales contain the same notes).

You'll notice there isn't a work in this book written in the key of F major (i.e. there is no *Etude in F*). Writing a work in the key of D minor – which we learned has the same notes as the key of F – means we already have a work in that key. The underlying principle of this book is: **each work is in a different key.**

There are 12 keys – hence 12 works.

In the simplest terms:

Each work is composed using a different set of notes.

(Consider the above a very brief outline and in no way a complete description of the concept of keys/ key signatures.)

PAGE LAYOUT

Page layout can be very important when learning a piece. If you have a piece where the first section is 8 bars long, it would be illogical to have 7 bars on the first page, and the 8th bar on the next page. It would break the musical cohesion of the section, and of the work as a whole.

Layout affects how a work is read and, consequentially, how a work is learned. Lots of bars squashed together would be off-putting, as the music would have no visual structure or appeal. The equivalent would be reading a novel consisting entirely of sentences, with no paragraph breaks etc.

The material itself may be fantastic, but the layout could/would detract from the context.

Many composers write works with strict bar phrasing, i.e. a work may solely consist of 4-bar phrases. The most logical layout in such an instance would be 4 bars per line. An illogical layout would be 3 bars in the first line, followed by 4 bars per line thereafter. Such a layout would affect the readability of the musical material, and affect the sense of continuity in learning and playing the work.

With these *Etudes*, special consideration has been given to layout. Each page of each piece can be viewed as a section of the piece as a whole. The page turns are at musically logical changes of section. If you're intending to commit any of the *Etudes* to memory, the page turns will more than likely be the 'memory chunk' transitions (i.e. the points where you'd naturally split the music in order to memorise it).

In some instances you'll see repeat signs, and in other instances there are no repeat signs where there could be repeat signs. This is intentional.

In *Etude in D*, page 1, bars 5-8 are an exact repeat of bars 1-4. On page 2, bars 13-16 are an exact repeat of bars 9-12. Both sections could have been written with repeat signs, but for me, clear 8-bar sections per page are easier to read/follow (in the instance of this specific work). The music, in this specific instance, 'reads' better without repeat signs.

As stated above, not all repeat signs are omitted: in *Etude in Gm*, you'll notice the first 4 bars are repeated. Again, this is to maintain the integrity of each page.

The aim is **consistency with respect to readability of musical material.**

LEFT-HAND FINGERING

LH (left-hand) fingering is one of the most important aspects of learning and playing a piece. The fingers we use have direct impact on whether a piece is easy, difficult, or impossible to play.

Ironically, only a handful of electric guitar books include fingering. We could practise a certain section of a work with a specific fingering, only to later realise there are more effective fingerings than the fingering we ourselves used.

This can be very frustrating, as we have to *unlearn* what we've learned. Many guitarists understandably don't bother unlearning, and make the most of the fingering they utilised in the first place.

This is no fault of the guitarist: given most books have no fingering, the guitarist has to work out a systematic fingering of their own, and on their own.

It also isn't the fault of the artist: most artists are simply too busy performing to create detailed scores of their music (and in many instances, entire sections of their music are improvised).

To look at the issue from the other side: in many instances there can be a number of possible fingering solutions. To specify *only* one fingering could actually be limiting to the performer.

Another important point: we all have different-sized hands! A comfortable fingering for me could be impossible for you, and vice versa. The size of hand, length of fingers, span etc. all affect the possible ways in which we can/could play something.

In saying that, with my *Etudes*, I have specified all fingering. There are four main reasons for this:

1) **Time.** Specified fingering will save the guitarist valuable time learning/unlearning possible fingering patterns.

2) **Playing smoothly.** Many passages can only be played smoothly with the specified fingering: to deviate from it is more likely to produce a break in sound.

3) **Use of the 4th finger.** Many guitarists avoid using the 4th finger. The result of this can be very limiting. Certain passages of the *Etudes* have been written in such a way that the only possible fingering solution to enable playing smoothly requires use of the 4th finger.

4) **Equality of LH finger strength/activation.** The following is possibly slightly too technical for a book such as this (i.e. a book with focus on the music and not structure of the music), but given its technical importance, I believe it is worth mentioning. Prior to composing the *Etudes,* a number of algorithms were devised which would, when implemented, guarantee a *minimum frequency occurrence* of each finger. I like to call this the *frequency floor*. The frequency floor of each finger was calculated to be a ratio of the length of each piece, and the use of each finger in each piece is itself a ratio of all 12 works as a whole. In plain English: let's assume a piece is 100 notes long. If each finger was given a frequency floor of 15%, each finger would be used at *least* 15 times in the 100-note piece. The other, 'spare' notes (in this instance, 40 other notes), could be shared across all fingers (giving our piece total equality in terms of finger activation), or the remainder could primarily be devoted to a single finger/set of fingers (i.e. we could devote 30 of our 40 remainder notes to finger 3, or share the remainder notes between fingers 3 and 4). What is created with such an approach are works that can either a) have equal activation of every finger, or b) be devoted primarily to the activation of a specific finger/ specific fingers. Key to this approach is as follows: even if we choose to focus on strengthening one specific finger, all other fingers are still being used a minimum number of times, which guarantees an equality of technical development across the entire hand.

All pieces use every finger, and every finger is used in every piece a minimum number of times, with this minimum figure itself being a ratio of the length of the piece. In learning **any** *Etude*, you'll strengthen/ develop activation of *every* LH finger, with certain works developing every finger *plus* having a focus on a specific finger/specific fingers.

Also created were a number of algorithms to ensure all possible LH fingering permutations were used throughout the book. Again, in plain English: I could satisfy the 'minimum floor' principle with each piece, but fail to fully develop LH potential. For example: finger 3 could be used 20 times in a 100-note piece, but I may be, in every instance, moving to/from finger 3 to/from finger 1. This wouldn't really develop my technique, as I wouldn't be covering the entire spectrum of possible movements to/ from finger 3. To cover the entire spectrum, I'd need to make sure I was moving from an open string – finger 3, finger 3 – open string, finger 1 - finger 3, finger 3 - finger 1 etc. Simply 'using a finger more often than other fingers' won't adequately develop strength or independence, as strength/ independence is more effectively achieved through *Interdependence* (i.e. working each finger in relation to the other fingers, rather than working each finger as a 'single unit').

Over the course of the *Etudes*, every possible LH fingering permutation is utilised. The frequency occurrence of each permutation is also calculated as a ratio of the entire book.

So, what's the point of all this underlying structure? The point is this – no possible fingering permutation is omitted and no finger is given precedence over any other finger. The result = this set of works will take your playing as close as is mathematically possible to achieving complete LH finger independence/ interdependence.

Such an approach removes potential 'composer bias'. If a composer has a slight weakness in, for example, their 2nd finger, there's a good chance when writing pieces they'd utilise the 2nd finger less than the other fingers. This will have an effect on the musical outcome.

Given these *Etudes* are written as technical studies, having a compositional bias would actually be detrimental to the aim of the book. The underlying structural principles used throughout the book guarantee a level of purity and completion that couldn't be achieved otherwise.

***

Some of the specified fingering may, at first sitting, feel 'odd'. In most instances, the fingering I've added is actually the *easiest* way to play the music smoothly. In other instances, the fingering serves a specific technical purpose (see the section on *Backstepping* as an example of this).

You can, of course, choose your own fingering for each piece. However, I'd actively encourage learning each work with the specified fingering before trying your own fingering. In trying your own fingering, you may miss some of the technical difficulties of the *Etudes*; technical difficulties that will add benefit to your playing. You also may inadvertently build a 'finger bias' into your hand.

Take note that if, in a work, a bar/section is repeated with the same fingering, the fingering is only added in the first bar/section. If there is no fingering, the fingering is the same as when the passage previously occurred.

Let's illustrate this point by looking at *Etude in D.* Bars 1 and 2 are the same material – the fingering has only been added in bar 1, as bar 2 has the same fingering:

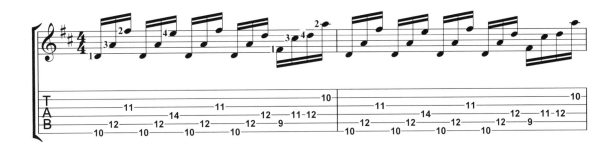

Bars 41 and 42 are exact repeats of bar 1, hence no fingering in these bars:

This lack of fingering on the score doesn't mean 'use any finger you want' – it means the passage has occurred previously in the music, and we are to use the same fingering as before.

In the above examples, the fingering is the same for every bar.

Note that throughout the book, LH fingering is written on the musical staff, and not on the TAB. Fingering added to TAB would be too confusing: we could, in some instances, confuse fingering for frets/frets for fingering. You don't necessarily have to be able to read notated music; you can simply look up from each TAB note to the musical staff to see which finger to use.

BACKSTEPPING

Have a look at the following example:

Can you think of any LH fingering that would allow us to play smoothly between the notes?

Trying to play the above example perfectly smooth creates difficulties in terms of fingering. The 'standard' fingering solution would most likely be as follows:

But this fingering isn't ideal, as we have to 'jump' between fingers 2 and 4. Unless your fingers are extremely long, it'll probably be impossible for you to play the above example smoothly.

If the example was rewritten at the 1st fret, it would now be completely impossible to play smoothly between the final two notes:

A possible solution to the first example could be barring both 7th fret notes:

Whilst a reasonable solution, it isn't ideal, as the simple act of barring means we'll spill the notes over each other. This will affect the sense of *melody*, as we'll now be perceiving two notes at once, rather than one note at a time. There is a place for this technique (i.e. we commonly find it in Blues music), but in a purely melodic phrase, it is probably more detrimental than beneficial to the overall sound.

The above examples don't mean it is impossible to play smoothly between these notes – they simply mean that *it is impossible to play smoothly with the standard fingering, as outlined above.*

Have a look at the fingering in the following example, which solves the problem:

We can now play perfectly smoothly between the notes.

We found our solution with a technique known as *backstepping*. Backstepping is a simple term, meaning *to place a finger behind a higher finger.* The technique is most often found with notes at the same fret. In the above example, finger 1 backstepped finger 2. The backstepping allowed us to stretch to the 11th fret without any break between notes.

It would be rare to encounter a backstepped chord, as the technique is more often used to play smoothly in single-note passages. However, for the sake of completion, let's have a look at the technique in a chordal context:

Here is an A chord with standard fingering:

And here is a backstepped A chord:

The backstepped A chord feels very alien. Such fingering is rarely encountered, but does, in certain instances, have its place.

Backstepping is relatively rare in electric guitar music, but is frequently found in classical guitar music. The primary reason for its relative obscurity in electric guitar music possibly has more to do with lack of awareness than a conscious decision to dismiss the technique, given it does serve a very useful purpose.

You'll find numerous examples of backstepping throughout these *Etudes* (especially so in *Etude in G#m*, which is, on one level, a partial study of the technique): don't worry, the fingering isn't wrong – the backstepping simply offers a solution to the problem of playing smoothly between certain notes.

Try incorporating backstepping in your own playing/writing – you'll find it may allow you, in certain instances, to play far smoother and cleaner.

Note that the inverse of backstepping i.e. **Overstepping** – can also be found throughout the book.

RIGHT–HAND PICKING

This book focuses exclusively on the right–hand picking technique known as **alternate picking**. Alternate picking is very simple in concept: when picking, we *alternate* between downstrokes (Π) and upstrokes (V). We'd be thinking 'down, up, down, up' etc.

Using the downstroke/upstroke symbols, alternate picking would look like this:

Π V Π V Π V Π V etc.

Here is the open 3rd string, alternate picked:

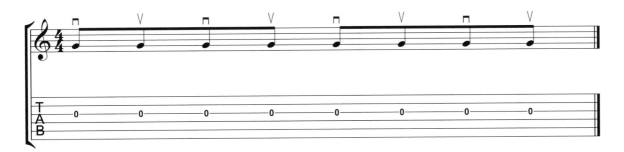

(Note that in almost every instance of alternate picking, we begin on a downstroke.)

Alternate picking can be subdivided into various categories. The above example is what we would call **Single-String Picking**. We call it single-string picking as we are picking on one string.

Another category of alternate picking is ***Cross-Picking*** (Cross-picking – note the hyphen – shouldn't be confused with ***Crosspicking***, which is a separate technique).

In simple terms, cross-picking is picking across the strings. Below is an example of cross-picking:

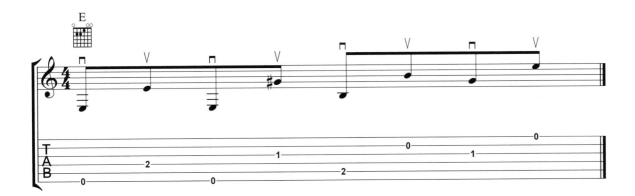

We are still alternate picking, but now across the strings.

If we take a standard scalar run, in terms of RH it contains both single-string picking and cross-picking:

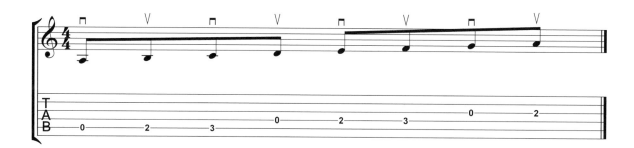

Here is the same example, this time with the sections of single-string picking and cross-picking indicated (the single-string picking is indicated within the ellipses, and the cross-picking is indicated within the rectangles):

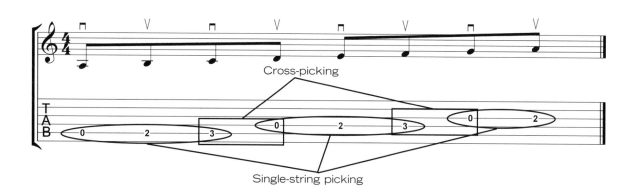

Let's have a closer look at some potential difficulties associated with cross-picking. The following example should feel easy enough:

However, this example will feel 'awkward':

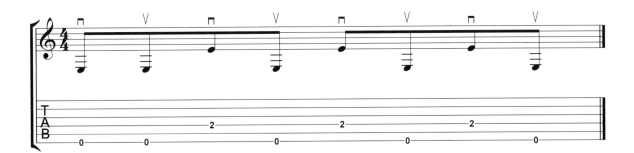

(Make sure you pick exactly as written.)

Let's exaggerate this by playing on the 6th and 1st strings. We'll begin easy:

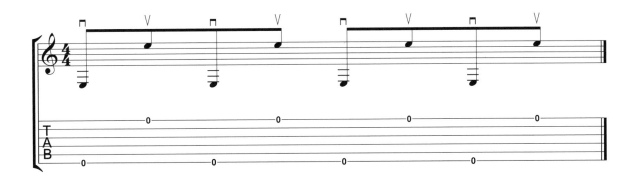

Contrast the above with the following very awkward exercise, which feels almost 'alien' as a product of the alternate picking:

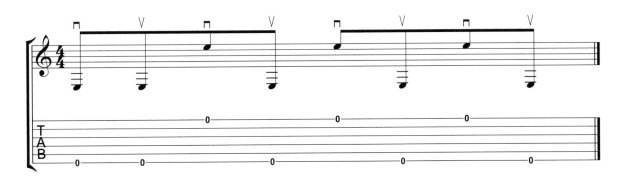

Cross-picking can, in certain instances, be very easy, and yet in other instances very tricky indeed. There's obviously more to cross-picking than simply 'picking across the strings'.

Let's have a closer look at the key components of cross-picking: two techniques we refer to as

Inside Picking and **Outside Picking.**

INSIDE/OUTSIDE PICKING

Of the two techniques, outside picking is by *far* the easier of the two.

Outside picking is **picking the outside of two strings.** What do we mean by 'inside' and 'outside'? Have a look at the following example:

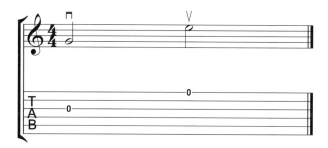

In the above example, we are picking the **outside** of both strings. Technically, when we pick the 3rd string with a downstroke, our hand falls lower – moving us toward the 1st string.

Let's invert the picking, and begin on an upstroke:

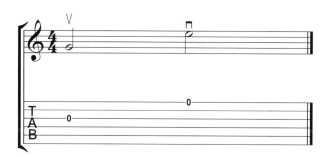

In this example, we are picking the *inside* of both strings. Picking the 3rd string with an upstroke moves our hand *away* from the string we intend to pick. This is the very essence of the difficulties associated with inside picking.

With outside picking, our hand moves <u>toward</u> the next string we are to pick.

With inside picking, our hand moves <u>away</u> from the next string we are to pick.

Hence inside picking is far more difficult: we are forced to move in the opposite direction from the direction in which our hand should travel.

The further apart the strings are, the more difficult inside picking becomes. Hold an E chord and try the following:

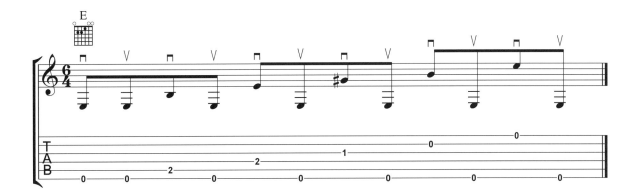

The RH picking of this exercise becomes progressively more difficult due to the string spacing becoming wider.

The most difficult inside picking we can encounter on a 6-string guitar is between the 6th and 1st strings. The easiest inside picking is between any adjacent strings, e.g. 6th and 5th, 5th and 4th etc.

If we are inside picking *and* our LH is busy, life can become very difficult.

The following example should illustrate this point:

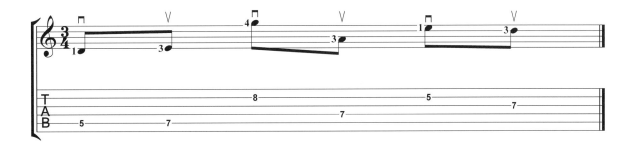

Here is an inside picking exercise between the 1st and 6th strings (i.e. the very threshold of difficulty in terms of inside picking) combined with tricky LH fingering: this exercise will lie anywhere, in terms of difficulty, between very tricky and borderline impossible, depending on the tempo you choose to play at:

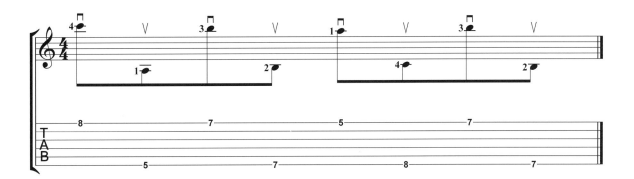

33

Exploration of this technique on 7/8/9 string guitar is untapped – and terrifying! On 9-string guitar, truly groundbreaking/impossible riffs could be constructed employing inside picking.

If we return to the scalar run we looked at earlier, we can now see that the two instances of cross-picking each employ a different technique - the first instance employs outside picking, and the second instance employs inside picking:

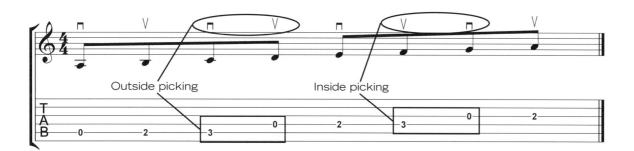

In terms of RH, the most difficult point of this bar will be the instance of inside picking.

One of the many benefits of understanding the subtleties of RH alternate picking is the ability to identify difficulties before picking up our instrument.

If you practise scales often, you'll probably find the most difficult RH points are where you encounter inside picking. You'll probably also find the same when looking through any tunes/solos you can play.

Isolating difficulties in such a way allows the difficulties to be exposed: once exposed (and understood), the difficulties can be *mastered*. The Etudes in this book contain *every* possible RH difficulty to be found in cross-picking.

To recap:

Alternate picking consists of two categories:

1) **Single-string picking**

2) **Cross-picking**

Cross-picking – a subset of alternate picking – consists of two categories:

1) **Outside picking**

2) **Inside picking**

This gives us three possible categories of alternate picking:

1) **Single-string picking**

2) **Inside picking**

3) **Outside picking**

From easy-difficult, our categories are ordered as follows:

1) **Single-string picking** (easiest)

2) **Outside picking**

3) **Inside picking** (most difficult)

Note there is no picking indicated on the *Etudes:* this doesn't mean 'pick any way you wish' (which would render many of the difficulties obsolete) – there is simply no point of indicating the picking for every note of every piece when every piece is picked with strict alternate picking.

Begin each piece with a <u>downstroke</u>, and alternate pick throughout.

Be <u>highly</u> vigilant of your picking when playing these works.

TECHNICAL NOTES

Clarity

For each piece, **no LH note should be held over any other LH note.** Be especially watchful of this with your 3rd and 4th fingers: many guitarists commonly hold these fingers over each other. Again, this is where practising slow is important. At speed, a 'spill' is difficult to notice. If you play too fast too early, you'll possibly spill, yet remain unaware, due to the notes moving so fast.

Be careful you don't head in the opposite direction and break between the notes. **Every LH note should be held until you play the next LH note.** Think of walking – when we put one foot on the ground, the other foot is raised. If we try to walk with two feet on the ground, we'll fall forward. If we have no feet on the ground, we are floating!

Picking

Every piece should be picked with **strict alternate picking** (i.e. constant down-up-down-up). If the picking deviates from this, you'll miss the entire point of the etudes. Alternate picking gives the RH more difficulties than, say, economy picking – but this is the purpose of these etudes.

Be especially watchful of etudes with an odd number of notes in each bar (i.e. *Etude in Am*, which has 11 notes per bar) – the picking will reverse itself in each bar (i.e. bar 1 will begin with a downstroke, bar 2 with an upstroke etc.).

Palm Muting/Dynamics

Palm muting isn't indicated. Whether to palm mute (or not) is left to the discretion of the player. Every piece can be played with: no mute, muted throughout, or anywhere in between. Dynamics (i.e. how loud/ soft to play) haven't been added. Again, feel free to do your own thing.

Open String Spill

This is a more subtle problem than the 'clarity' issue. In short, if you have an open string followed by a fretted note, make sure to cut off the open string when you play the fretted note. This is often referred to as *Dampening*.

Dampening is often achieved by:

1) Touching the previous open string with a free finger when fretting a new note, or

2) Using the inside of the finger holding the fretted note to cut off the previous open string.

'1' is commonly used when skipping strings, and '2' is commonly used when moving to a lower string adjacent to the open string just played.

THE ETUDES

ETUDE IN D

Many composers describe the key of D major as being 'bright' and 'joyful'. Of course, tempo/dynamics etc. will also have an influence on whether or not we perceive something as 'bright' or 'joyful', but in the instance of *Etude in D* bright and joyful are very fitting terms.

Bars 33-40 are great fun to play, and cover a considerable area of the neck across a relatively limited number of bars.

Bars 37-40, being high up the neck and consisting entirely of major arpeggios (D, A, and G major), will sound very bright – and would anyway, irrespective of key. These bars are possibly the brightest of the entire book.

Tip – music written in the high register and consisting entirely of major harmony will sound bright (you don't have to be in the key of D – but allegedly it can help!). If you add 'fast' to the mix (fast rhythms and/or fast tempo), your compositions will sound very bright indeed.

Great examples of 'high & major' are the opening guitar riff of Guns n' Roses 'Sweet Child o' Mine', and the opening piano riff of Vanessa Carlton's 'A Thousand Miles' – which possibly sounds the brighter of the two, given the faster rhythms.

Rhythmic Groupings

Bars 1-47: 3-3-3-3-4

Bar 48: 4-4-hold

Suggested Minimum Tempo – 4 notes per beat @ 82BPM

ETUDE IN D

MUSIC BY KRIS LENNOX

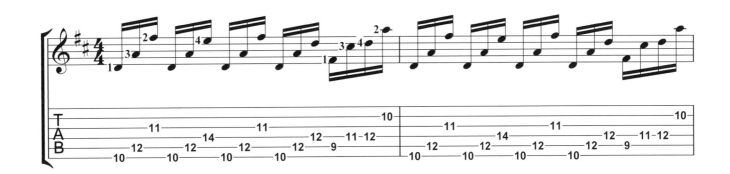

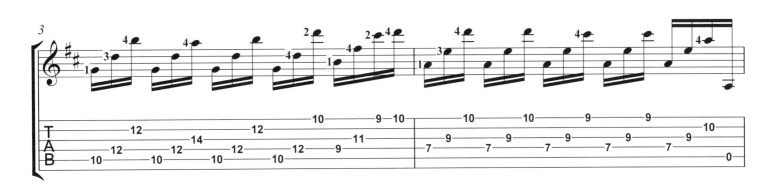

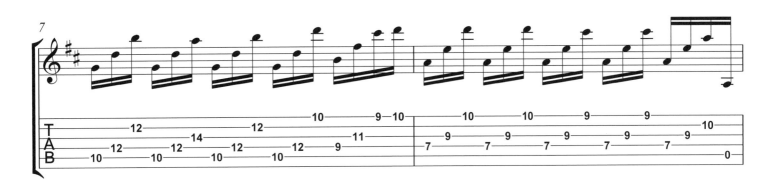

© Copyright 2015 Chester Music Limited.
All Rights Reserved. International Copyright Secured.

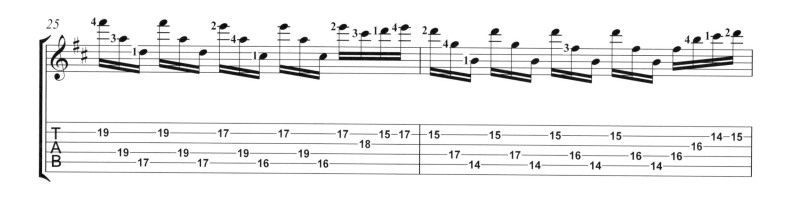

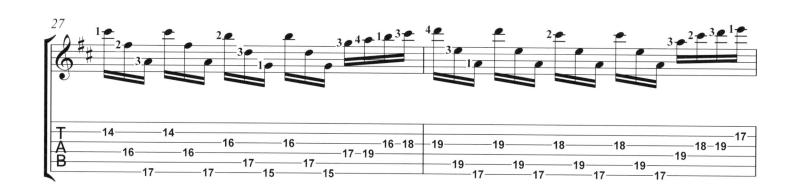

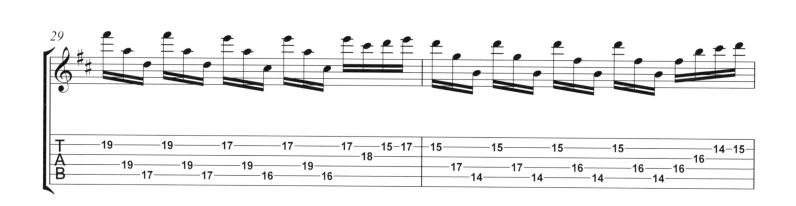

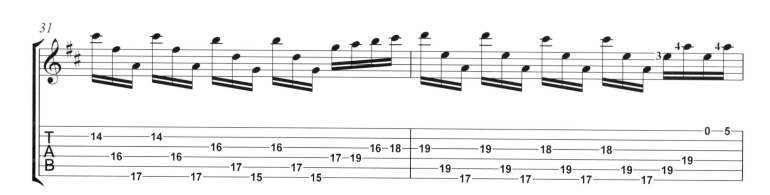

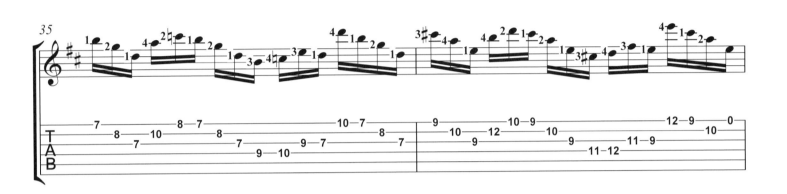

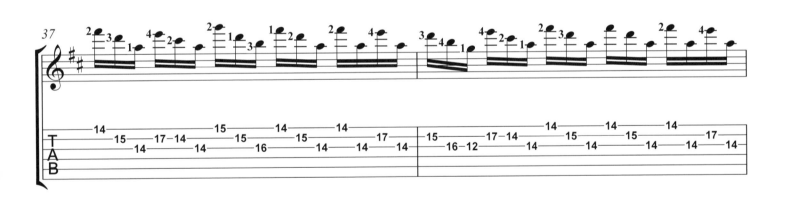

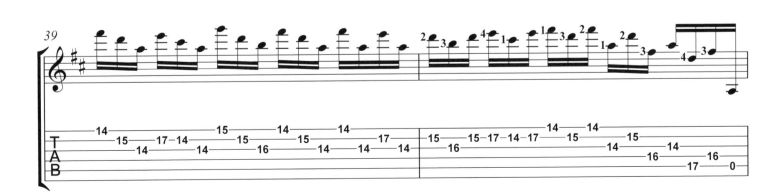

ETUDE IN Am

Etude in Am is, in terms of number of beats per bar, the most unusual work in this book. It has a time signature of 11/16, meaning there are 11 semiquavers in each bar. Take note that 11 is a prime number: prime numbers are great tools for creating 'musical oddness'. You may be asking why they are great for creating oddness. There is a simple explanation.

4/4 sounds 'good' to our ear as our mind can subdivide 4 beats as being two groups of 2 beats (2+2=4). **Our brain can deconstruct the music to simple, repeated numeric groupings.** Any time signature with 6 beats in a bar is also reasonably acceptable, as our mind can deconstruct 6 beat groupings to consist of either two groups of 3 beats (3-3), or three groups of 2 beats (2-2-2).

Prime number time signatures are a problem as they can't be deconstructed to 2 or 3 beat groupings. 7 beats in a bar can be thought of as 2-2-3 (or any variation i.e. 2-3-2, or 3-2-2), but it can't be thought of in terms of just 3-beat groupings, or just 2-beat groupings. **The mind has difficulty holding patterns where the beat groupings change.**

To test this, try tapping your foot along with *Etude in Am*. It is, at first try, very unnatural!

In terms of harmony, this work will sound, in places, Neoclassical. The Neoclassical sound (think Yngwie Malmsteen, and, to a point, Muse) can be created by using the *Harmonic Minor Scale*. In bar 44, we hear a clear example of the harmonic minor scale.

Tip – an odd number of beats in a bar will sound 'odd' to the ear. A time signature of 9/4 will sound less natural than 4/4. If you want to achieve the 'ultimate in oddness', have a prime number of beats in a bar (any prime number greater than 3). 5 beats in a bar will sound very odd to the ear, as will 7, 11, 13 etc.

Rhythmic Groupings

Bars 1-32: 4-4-3

Bar 33: 3-3-5

Bar 34: 5-3-3 (i.e. the inverse of the previous bar)

Bars 35-40: 3-3-5

Bars 41-end: 4-4-3

Suggested Minimum Tempo – 1 note per beat @ 340BPM

(This is the same as 2 notes per beat @170BPM (and 4 notes per beat @ 85BPM) – but this may prove more difficult to think, as every second bar will be off-beat.)

ETUDE IN Am

MUSIC BY KRIS LENNOX

© Copyright 2015 Chester Music Limited.
All Rights Reserved. International Copyright Secured.

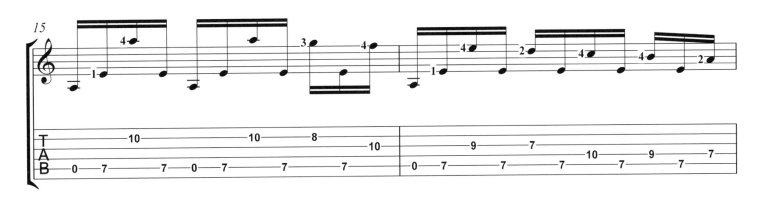

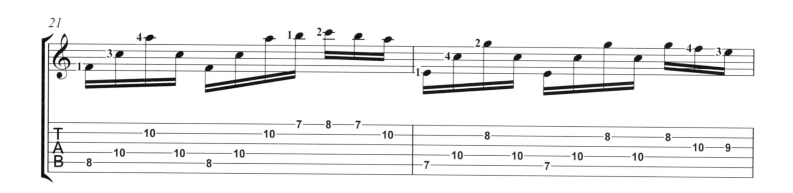

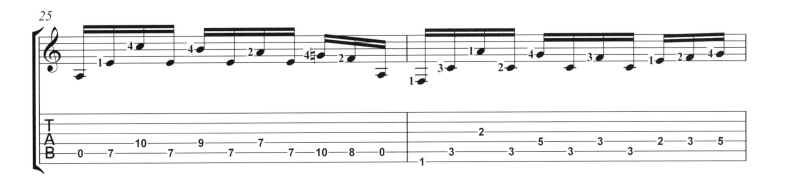

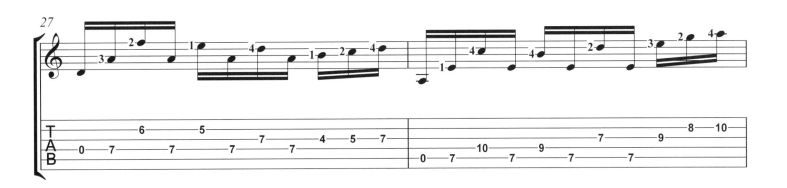

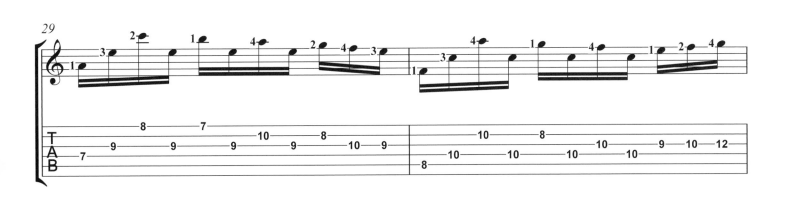

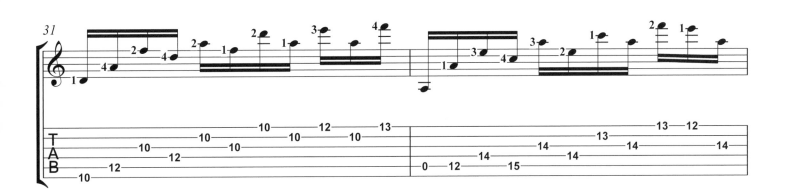

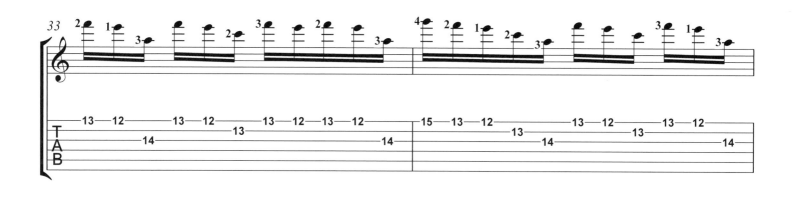

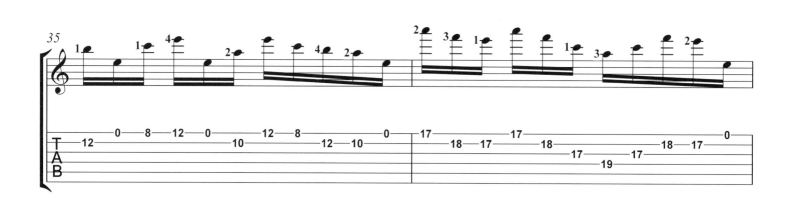

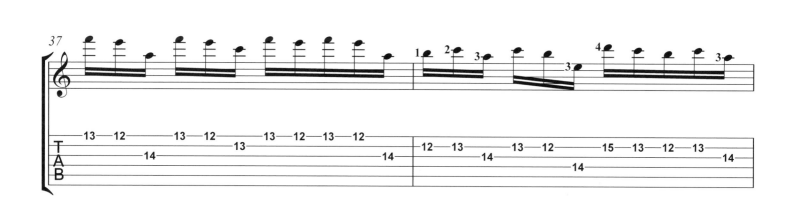

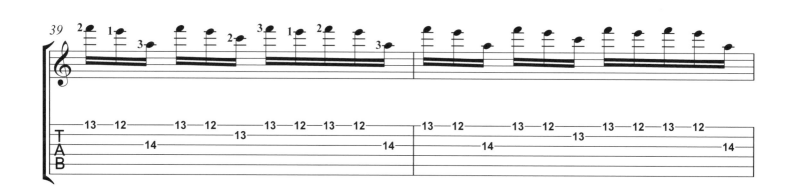

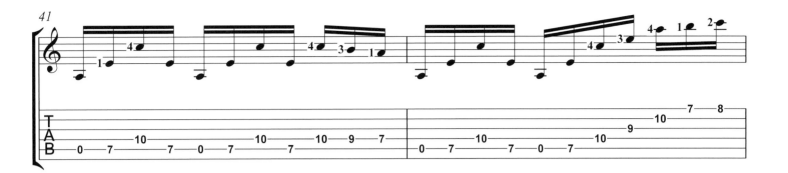

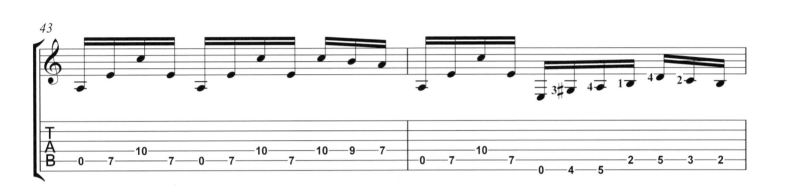

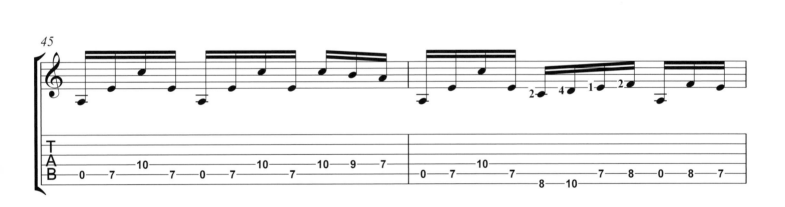

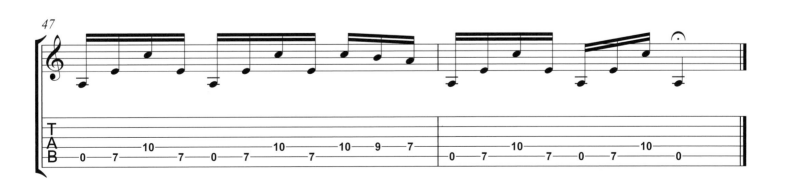

ETUDE IN E

52

Etude in E capitalises on four of the six open strings being notes from the key of E (6th, 5th, 2nd, and 1st strings). The initial bars demonstrate this, with frequent use of the open 1st and 2nd strings.

If you are familiar with Baroque music and are reminded of Bach when you first hear this work, congratulations, you have a great ear for pattern recognition! The initial phrase is a take on Bach's *Prelude in Cm,* from his *24 Preludes and Fugues.*

Tip – open strings are great for changing neck position fast and smooth. If you're looking to move up/down the neck quickly and are having trouble playing smoothly, look to see if any of the notes you are playing could be played on any of the open strings. If they can, you can use this open string as an opportunity to make a quick and clean LH position change.

Rhythmic Groupings

Bars 1-32: 4-4-4-4

Bars 33-36: 4-3-3-3-3

Bars 37&38: 4-4-4-4

Bars 39&40: 4-4-3-3-2

Bar 41-end: 4-4-4-4

Suggested Minimum Tempo – 4 notes per beat @ 84BPM

ETUDE IN E

MUSIC BY KRIS LENNOX

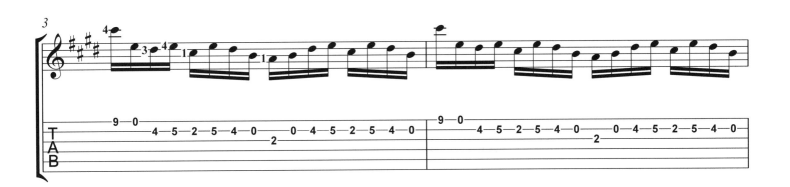

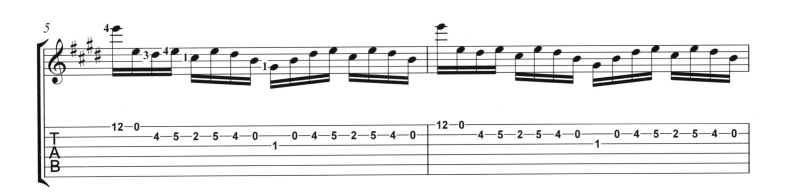

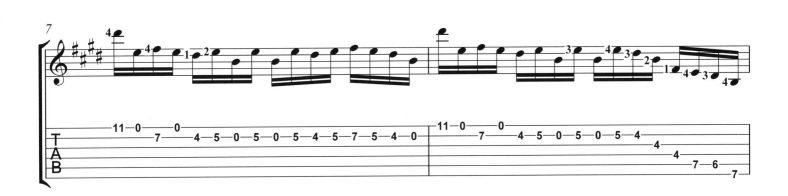

© Copyright 2015 Chester Music Limited.
All Rights Reserved. International Copyright Secured.

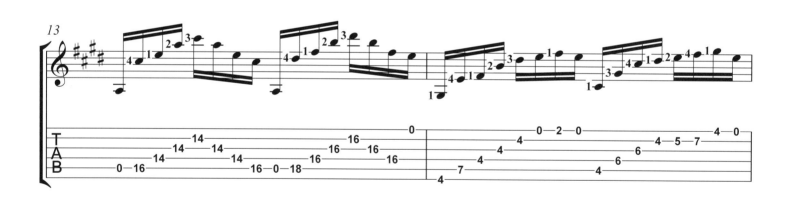

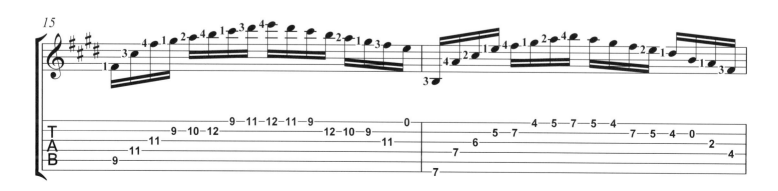

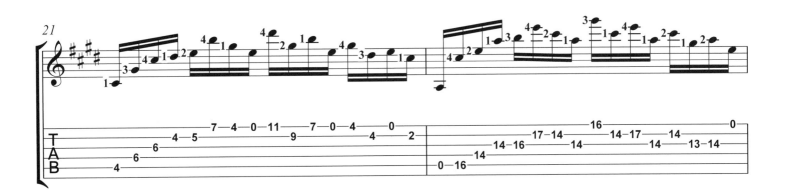

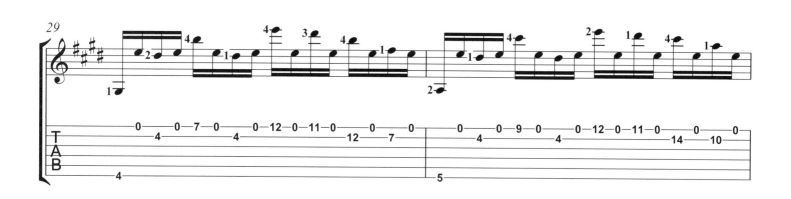

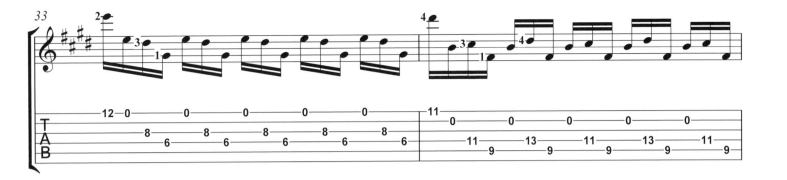

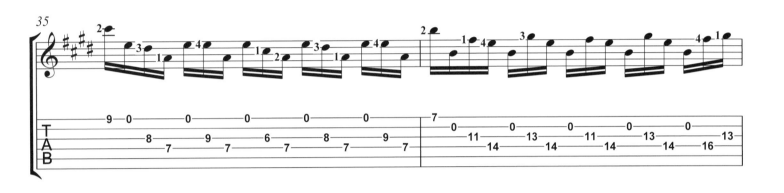

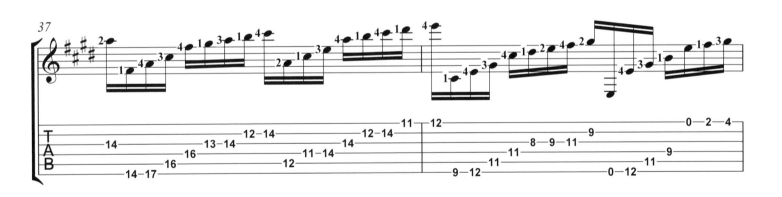

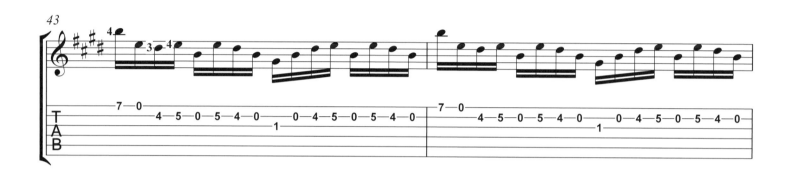

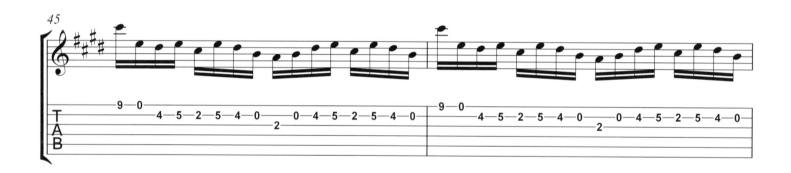

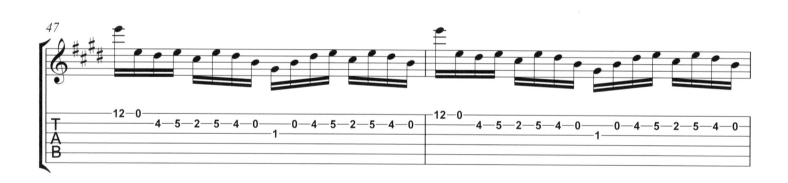

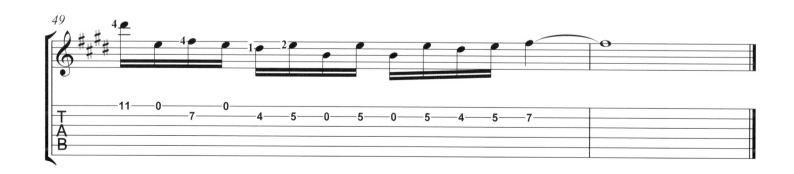

ETUDE IN E♭m

Etude in E♭m has very interesting – and often challenging – right hand string skipping sequences. In terms of the right hand, is this work as difficult as *Etude in Cm?*

The rhythmic groupings change often, throwing the sense of reference: just when it feels like a pattern is established, the patterns change! The continually shifting groupings should keep the mind as focused as the fingers.

Tip – changing the rhythmic groupings often can throw the listener's sense of reference and give your music an unpredictable quality. This is good <u>or</u> bad, dependent on the style of music you are composing. For a pop song, it could be disastrous!

Rhythmic Groupings

Bars 1-8: 4-4-4-4

Bars 9-16: 2-2-4-3-3-2

Bars 17-19: 4-4-4-4

Bar 20: 5-3-3-5

Bars 21-28: 4-4-4-4

Bar 29: 3-3-2-4-4

Bar 30: 3-3-6-4

Bar 31-end: 4-4-4-4

Suggested Minimum Tempo – 4 notes per beat @ 70BPM

ETUDE IN E♭m

MUSIC BY KRIS LENNOX

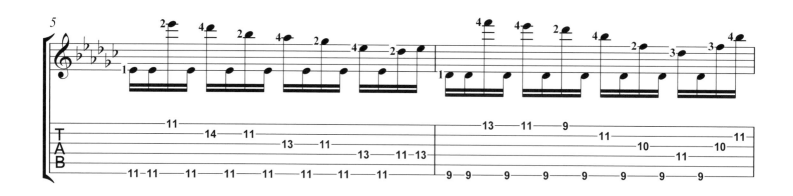

© Copyright 2015 Chester Music Limited.
All Rights Reserved. International Copyright Secured.

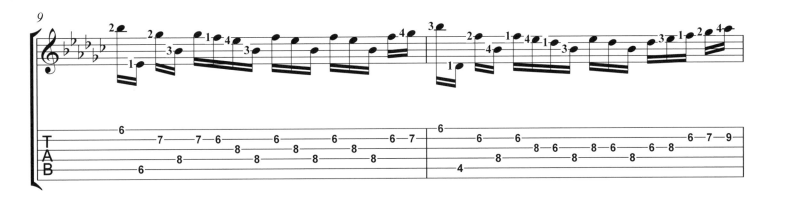

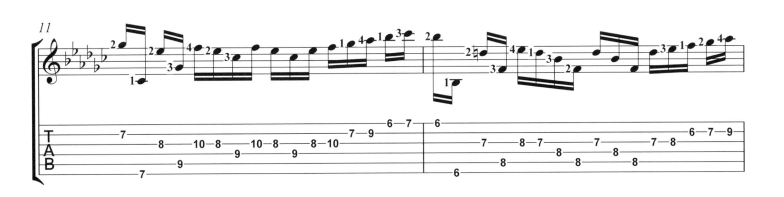

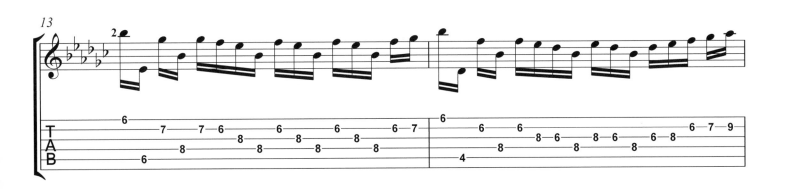

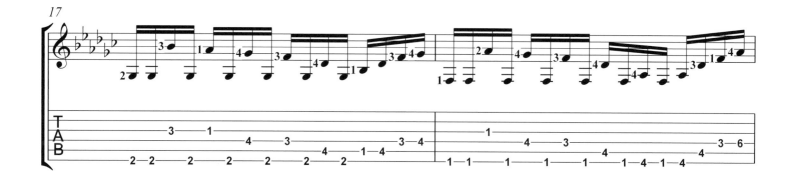

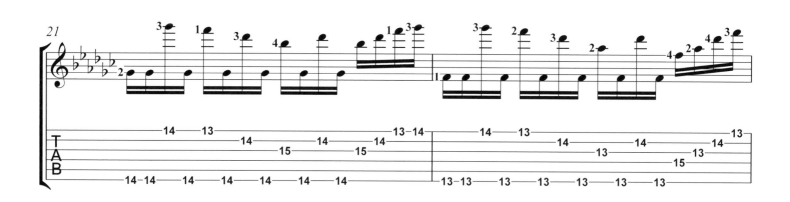

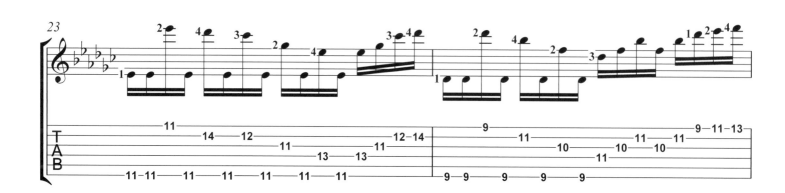

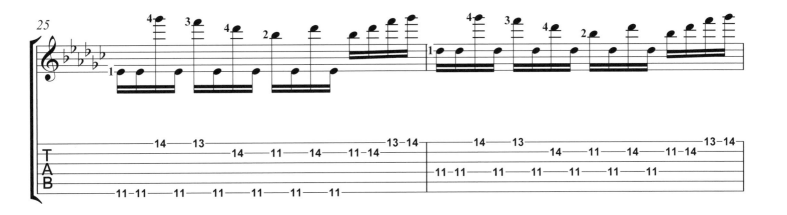

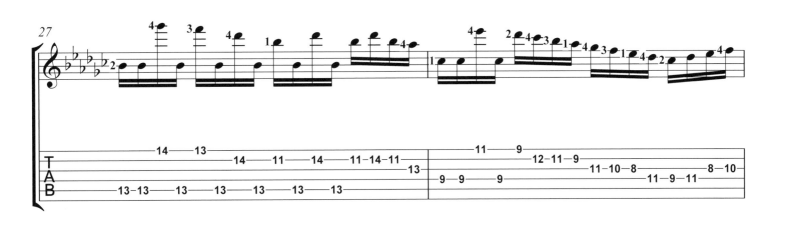

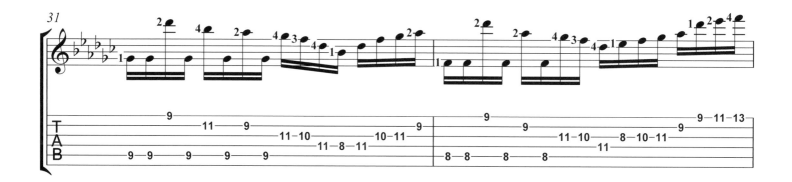

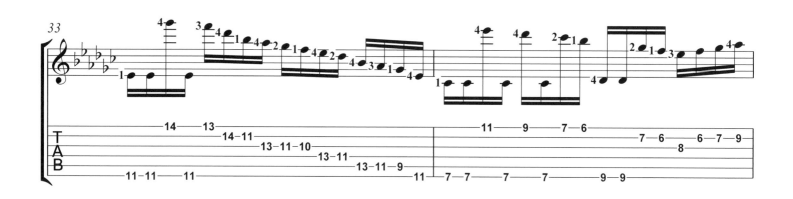

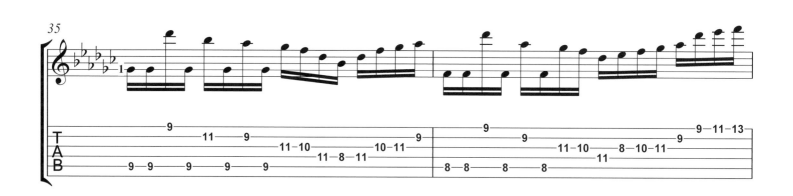

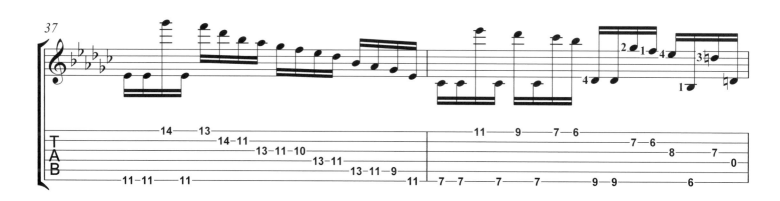

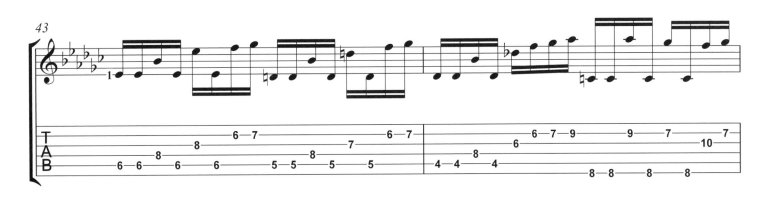

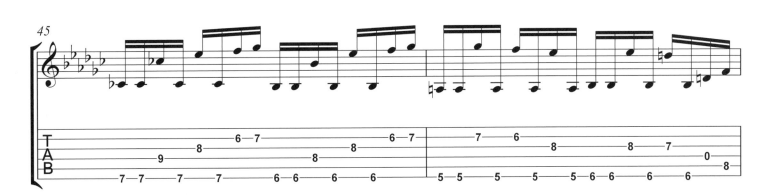

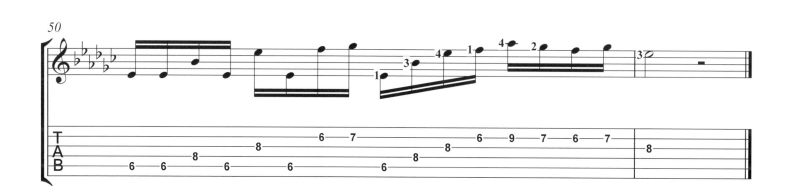

ETUDE IN B♭m

Etude in B♭m is possibly the most difficult LH work in this book. To play even the first two bars with clarity is a challenge in and of itself, let alone the entire piece. The fret coverage of page 1 will probably feel odd to most: upper reaches of neck, on every string. Covering the upper frets on the bass strings is relatively uncommon: don't be put off if the piece initially feels 'strange' as a consequence of this.

Tip – the upper frets on the bass strings aren't used in guitar music as often as other areas of the neck. There is potential for development of this area of the neck – whether in the form of solos, riffs, licks – or something else.

Rhythmic Groupings

Given all bars are only 6 quavers long, the rhythmic groupings can easily be thought of as 6-note groupings. If you'd prefer to subdivide certain bars (i.e. the first bar could be thought of as 3-3 or 2-2-2), by all means do so.

Suggested Minimum Tempo – 2 notes per beat @ 136BPM

ETUDE IN B♭m

MUSIC BY KRIS LENNOX

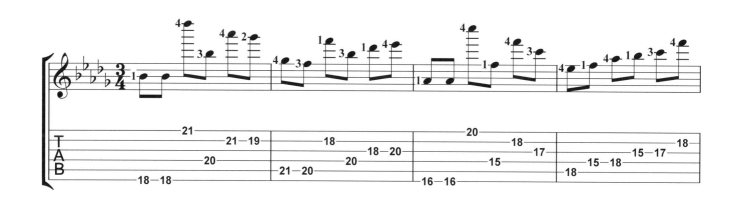

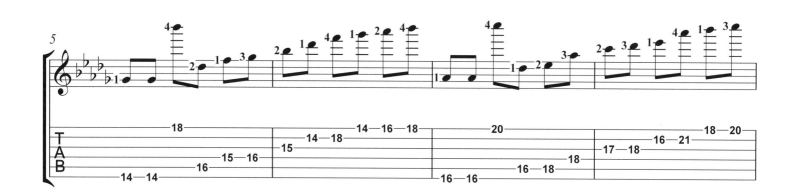

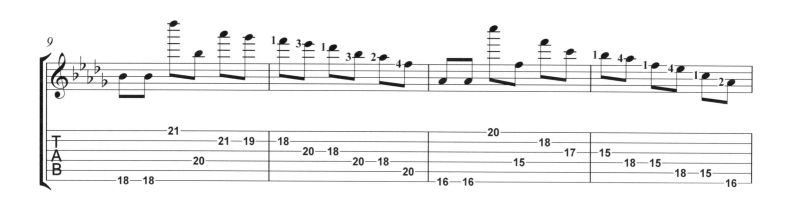

© Copyright 2015 Chester Music Limited.
All Rights Reserved. International Copyright Secured.

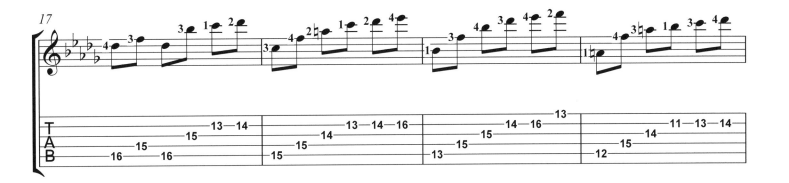

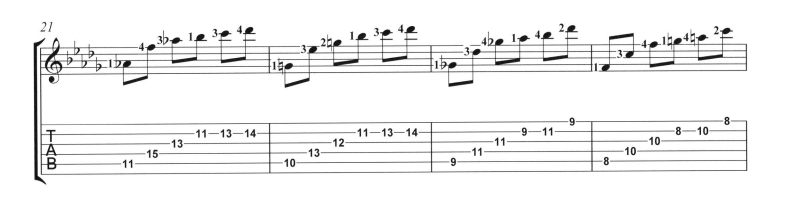

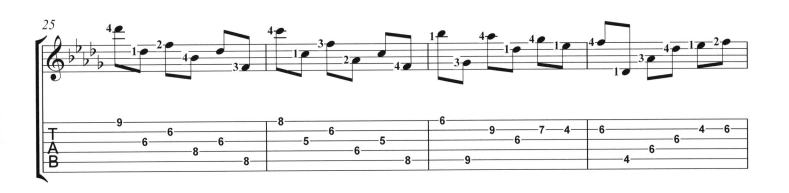

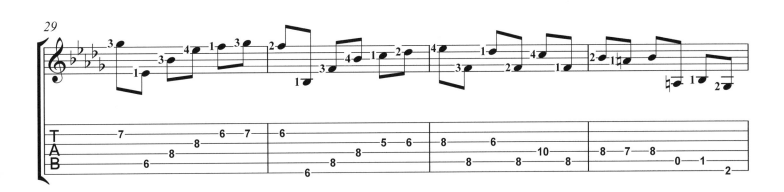

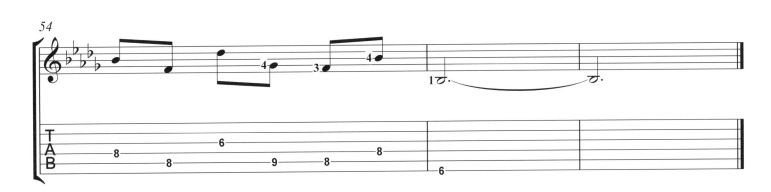

ETUDE IN Gm

72

Etude in Gm has a strong 'Rock' feel to it. The main theme (bars 1 and 2) is based on an arpeggiated G5 chord (i.e. a G5 power chord). Being a '5' chord, it is difficult to establish from the first two bars whether we are in a major or minor key. Bars 3 and 4 hint at minor, and in bar 5 we finally feel like we're in the minor key.

This piece is quite the workout! The repetition of the phrases demands good left hand stamina. Thankfully we have something of a LH break when we reach bar 25.

Tip – beginning a work on a power chord – either sustained or repeatedly played – is a great way of 'stalling' the sense of key. Power chords lack the '3rd' – the 3rd defines a chord as major or minor – this lack of a 3rd means the ear can't determine from the first chord if the work is in a major or minor key: this is a great tool for creating a sense of anticipation.

Rhythmic Groupings

Bars 1-28: 3-3-3-3-2-2 (or 3-3-3-3-4)

Bar 29: 4-4-4-4

Bar 30: 3-3-3-3-2-2

Bar 31: 4-4-4-4

Bar 32: 3-3-3-3-2-2

Bars 33-42: 4-4-4-4

Bars 43-46: 3-3-3-3-2-2

Bar 47: 5-5 (or 6-4)

Suggested Minimum Tempo – 4 notes per beat @ 90BPM

ETUDE IN Gm

MUSIC BY KRIS LENNOX

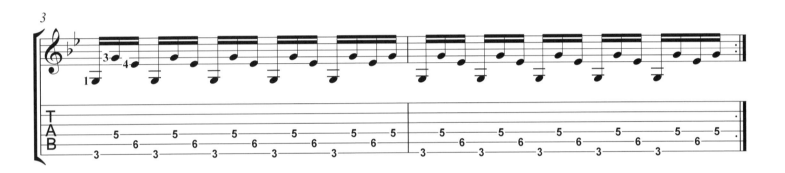

© Copyright 2015 Chester Music Limited.
All Rights Reserved. International Copyright Secured.

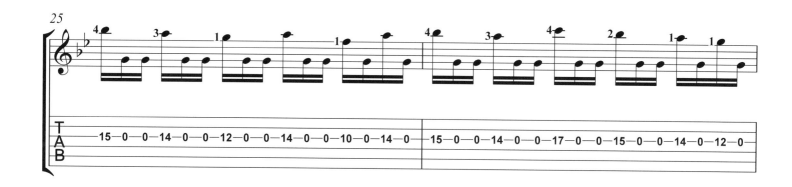

ETUDE IN Cm

79

There's no hiding from the fact that *Etude in Cm* is a right hand nightmare! The inside picking encountered in this work is very difficult indeed – and tiring. Is this technically the most difficult right hand work of the book?

Many of the left hand fingering sequences demand highly accurate finger placement/hand positioning: ironic, given the first page is, in terms of LH, relatively benign.

Tip – you'll probably be far more confident performing a work in front of an audience if you perform it slower than your threshold (e.g. 10% below your max tempo). However, many performers feel their best performances are when they are playing 'at the edge'. There are risks/benefits to playing safe, and risks/benefits to playing at the edge. It is up to you as a performer to decide on the best course of action. Beware the dangers of complacency - but also beware the trainwreck!

Rhythmic Groupings

Bars 1-15: 2-2-3-4-5

Bar 16: 2-4-4-6

Bars 17-23: 4-4-4-4

Bars 24-45: 2-2-3-4-5

Bar 46: 2-2-2-2-2-2-4

Bars 47&48: 4-4-4-4

Suggested Minimum Tempo – 4 notes per beat @ 80BPM

ETUDE IN Cm

MUSIC BY KRIS LENNOX

© Copyright 2015 Chester Music Limited.
All Rights Reserved. International Copyright Secured.

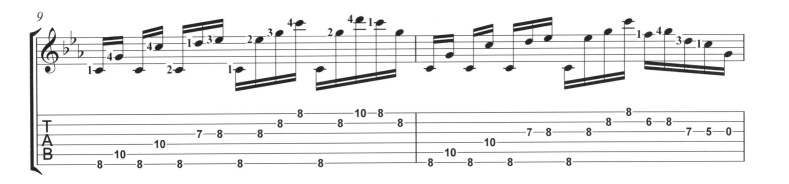

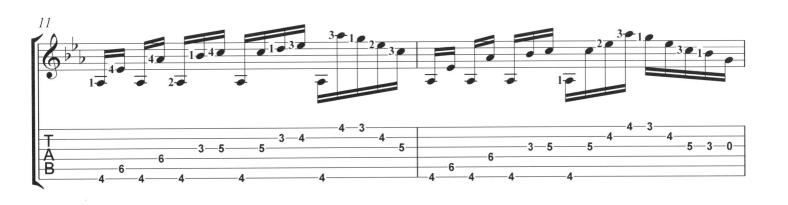

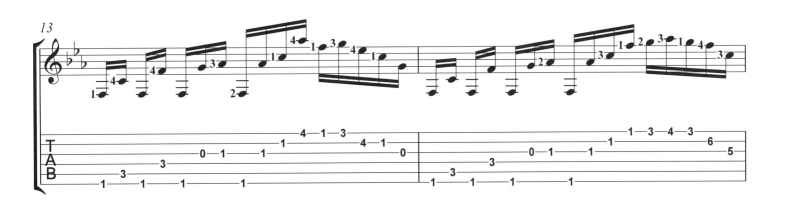

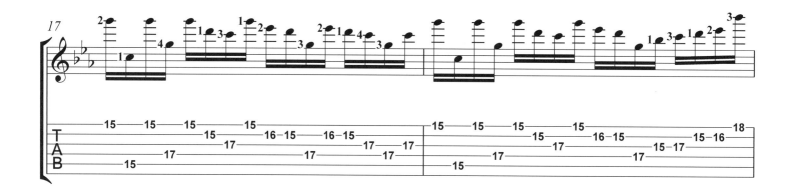

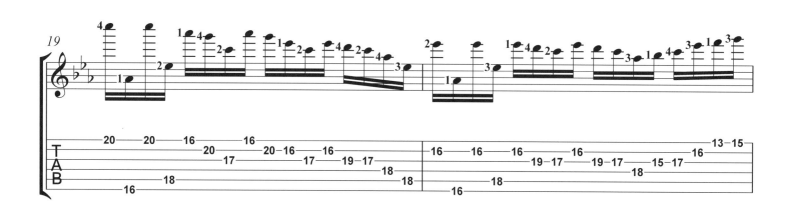

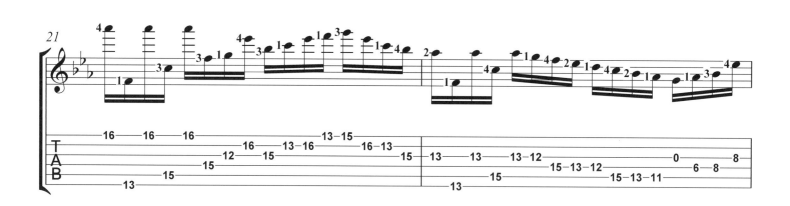

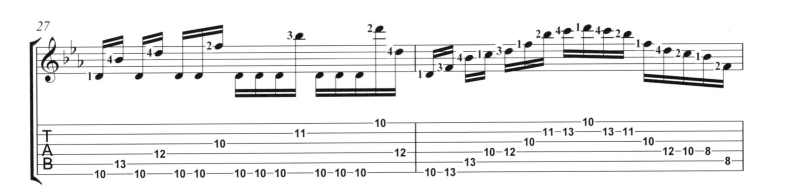

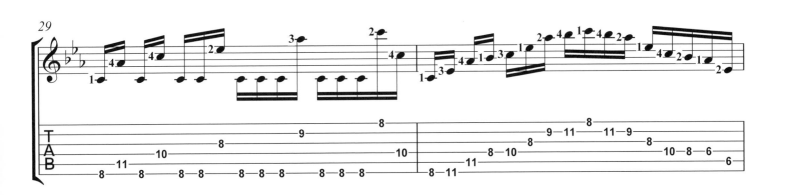

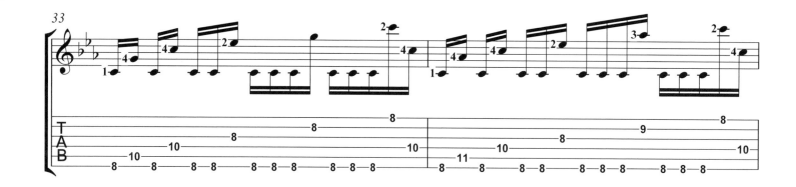

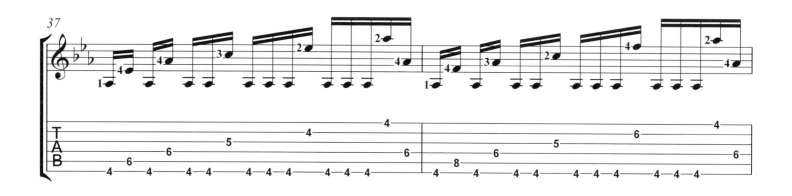

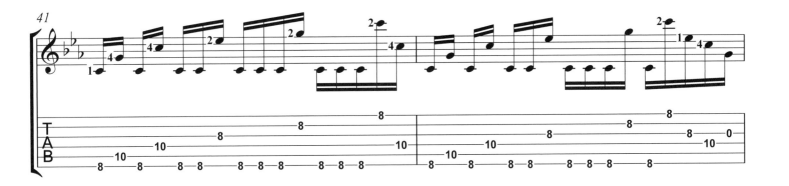

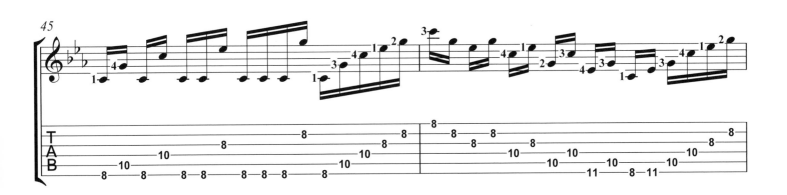

ETUDE IN A♭

Etude in A♭ plays with the idea of alternating between wide and narrow note ranges. This is very clear if we look at bars 1 and 2 (very wide note range) and compare them with bars 17 and 18 (very narrow note range).

Guitar music is rarely written in the key of A♭, which is unfortunate, as it has a very beautiful sound. The 19th century pianist/composer Franz Liszt would often use the key of A♭ when writing love songs.

Tip – the key of A♭ is widely held to be 'pretty to the ear'. If you intend to write a ballad/love song, it could be worth trying it in the key of A♭ to see if the key adds to the beauty.

Rhythmic Groupings

Bars 1-7: 4-4-3-3-2

Bar 8: 4-4-2-2-2-2

Bars 9-33: 4-4-3-3-2

Bar 34: 4-4-2-3-3

Bars 35-38: 4-4-3-3-2

Bars 39-41: 3-3-2

Suggested Minimum Tempo – 4 notes per beat @ 80BPM

ETUDE IN A♭

MUSIC BY KRIS LENNOX

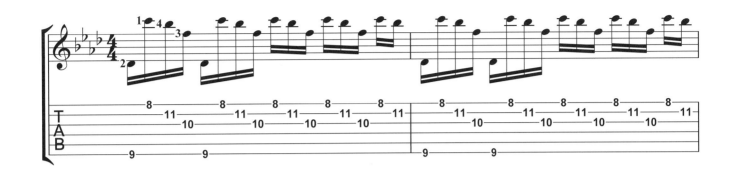

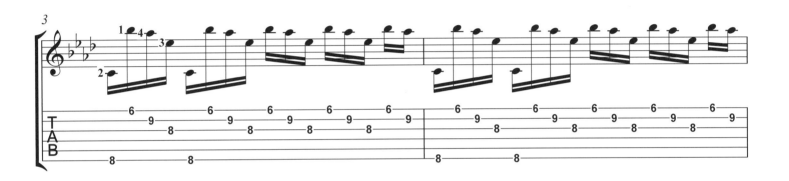

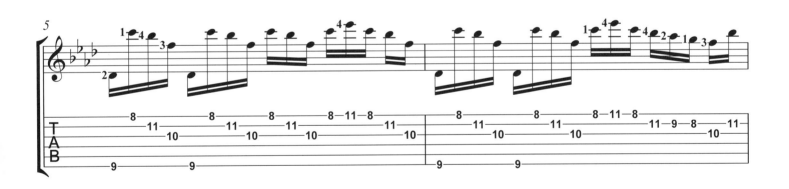

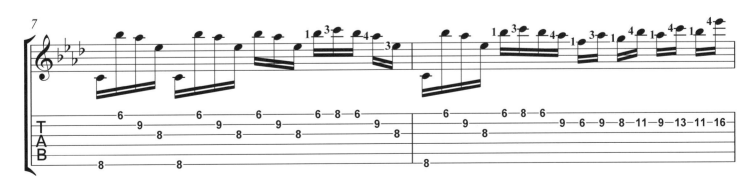

© Copyright 2015 Chester Music Limited.
All Rights Reserved. International Copyright Secured.

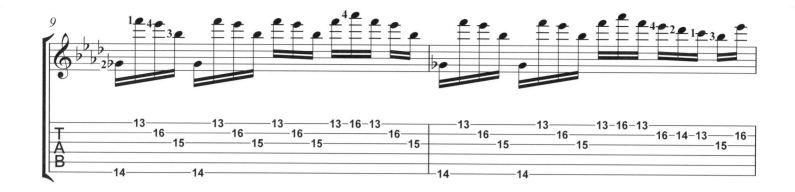

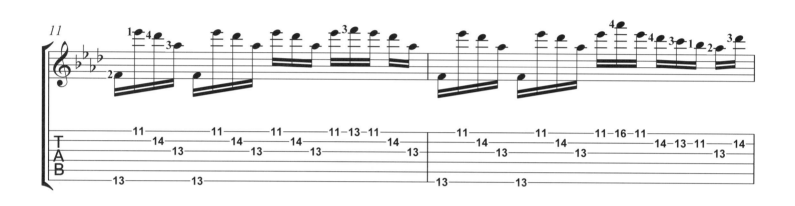

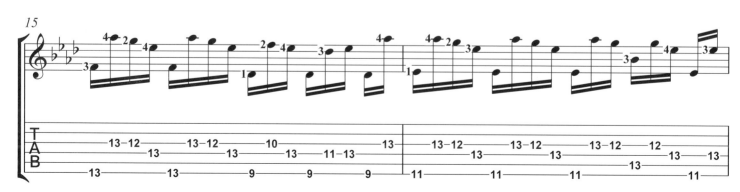

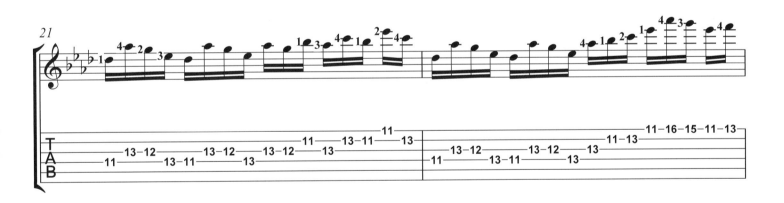

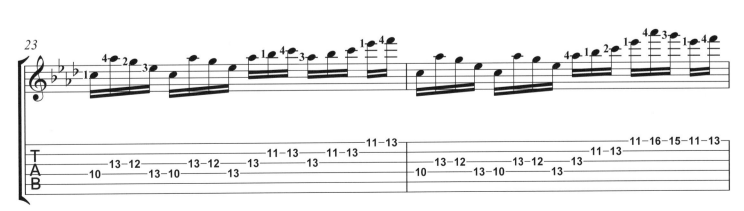

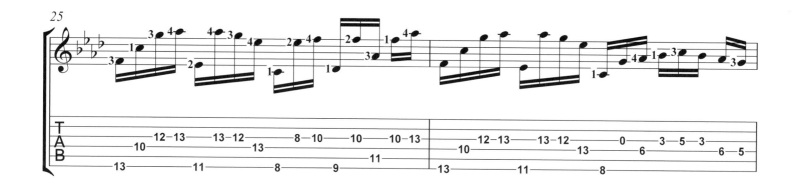

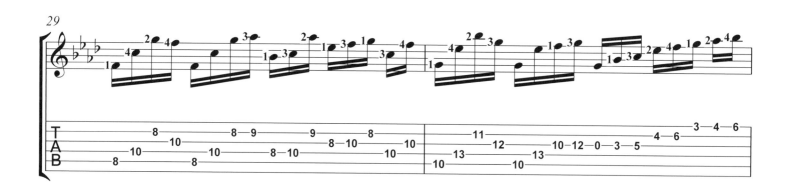

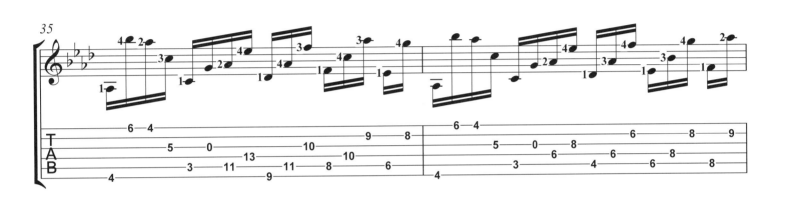

ETUDE IN G♯m

Perhaps the best words to describe *Etude in G♯m* are **awkward** and **unusual**. In both instances, this is intentional: the rhythmic groupings of 5-5-2-4 make the work awkward to practise with the metronome, and the harmony of the central section travels far from the key of G♯m, giving the work an unusual flavour. The frequent use of backstepping adds to the work's awkward and unusual nature. Bars 33-end sound less awkward than the rest of the piece – in these bars we find a more conventional sense of melodic movement, and the harmony stays exclusively in the key of G♯m.

Tip – odd rhythmic groupings can sound fantastic to the ear – as long as they sound intended and not accidental! Repeating an idea can make it sound intentional – playing an idea once can make it sound accidental. Repetition can be negative <u>or</u> positive – depending on context.

Rhythmic Groupings

Bars 1-8: 5-5-2-4

Bars 9-16: 5-7-4

Bar 17-end: 5-5-2-4

Suggested Minimum Tempo – 4 notes per beat @ 76BPM

ETUDE IN G#m

MUSIC BY KRIS LENNOX

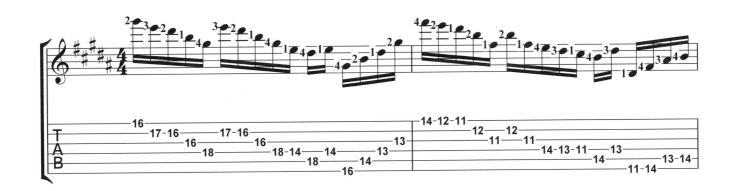

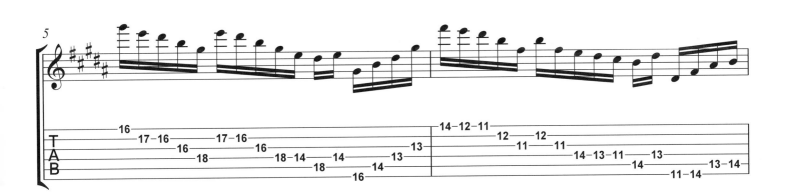

© Copyright 2015 Chester Music Limited.
All Rights Reserved. International Copyright Secured.

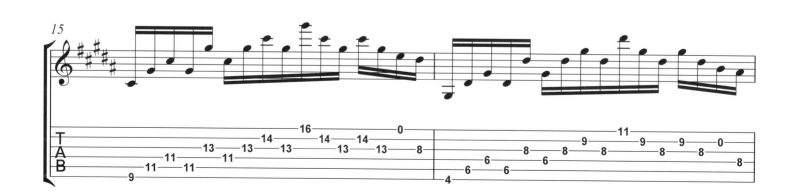

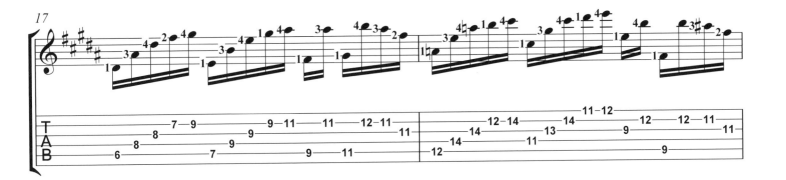

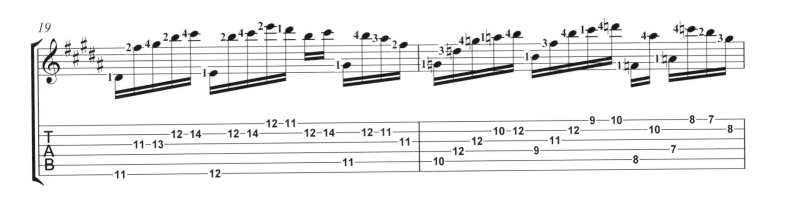

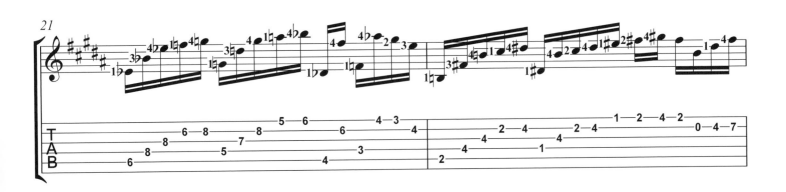

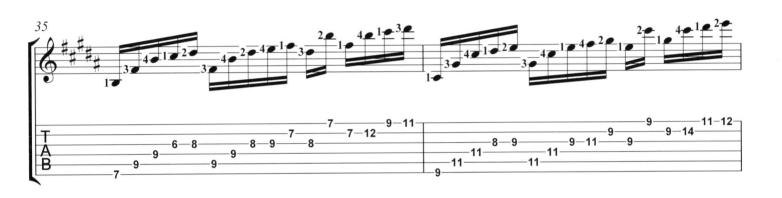

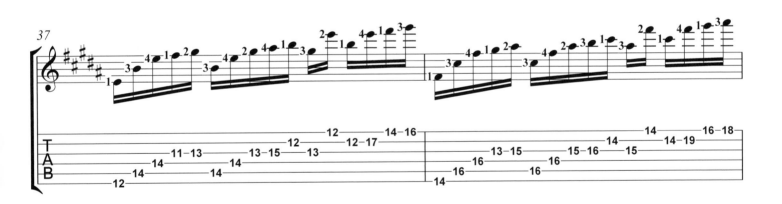

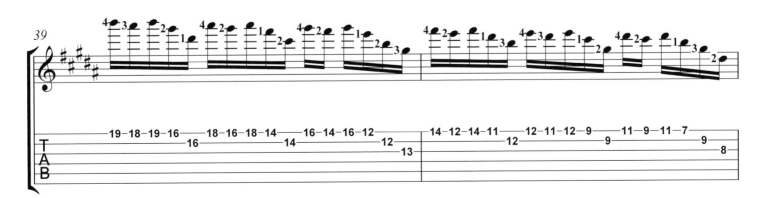

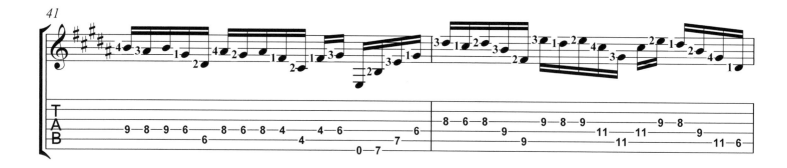

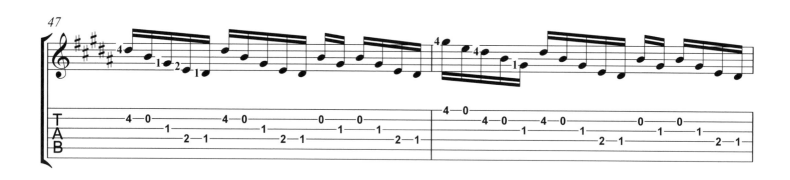

ETUDE IN Em

Etude in Em makes clever use of the open strings for changing left hand position quickly. The wide range covered in many bars creates a great sense of drama (in bar 1 alone we cover over 3 octaves, from open 6th string E to high G on the 1st string).

There are a number of 'jazzy' moments in this work, and also some quite unusual changes (i.e. the implied chord changes in bar 23).

Tip – to create a sense of wide emotional range in your compositions, cover a wide range in pitch.

Rhythmic Groupings

The entire work can be thought of as groupings of 4, i.e. 4-4-4-4 throughout, and 4-4 for the single bar of 2/4 at bar 36.

Suggested Minimum Tempo – 4 notes per beat @ 78BPM

ETUDE IN Em

MUSIC BY KRIS LENNOX

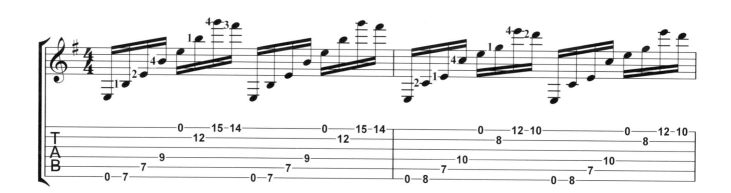

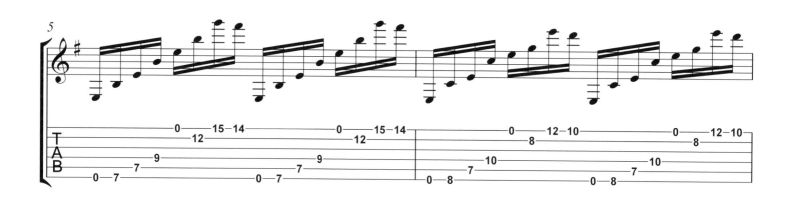

© Copyright 2015 Chester Music Limited.
All Rights Reserved. International Copyright Secured.

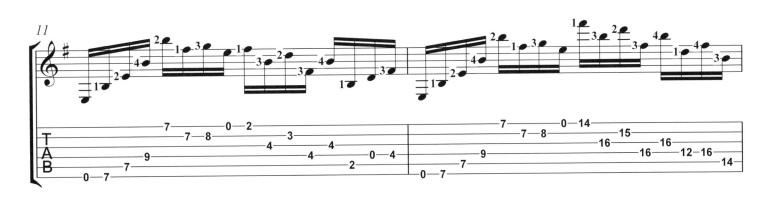

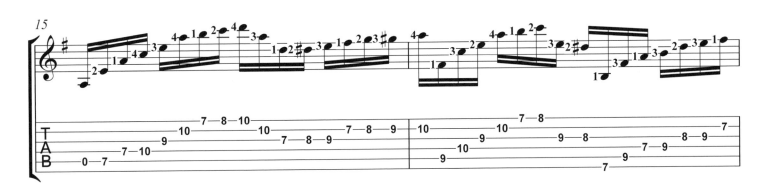

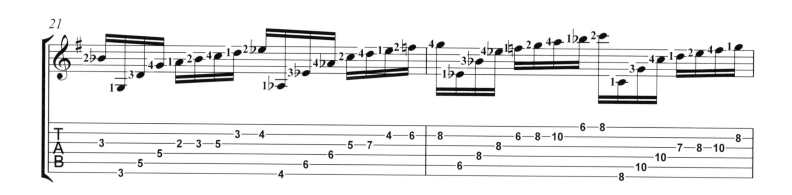

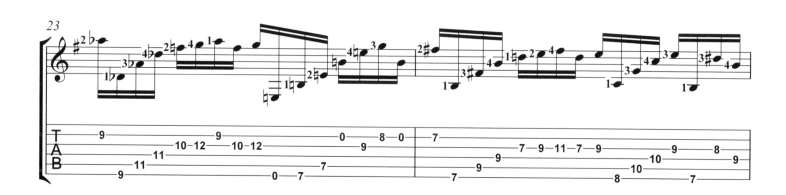

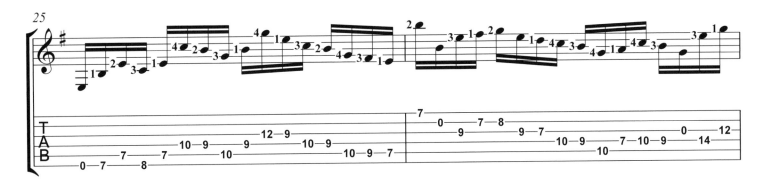

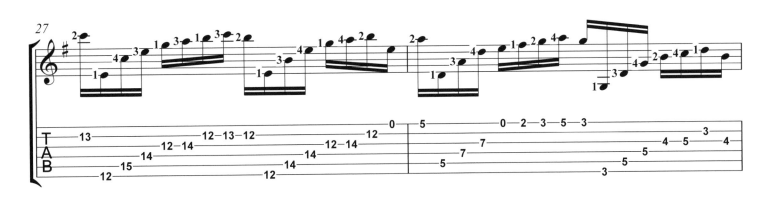

103

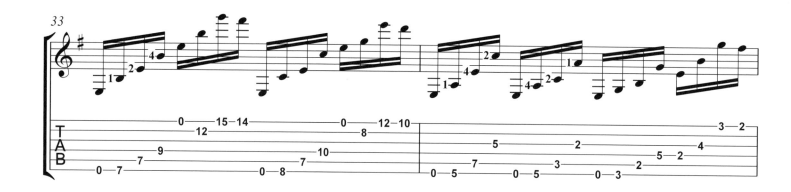

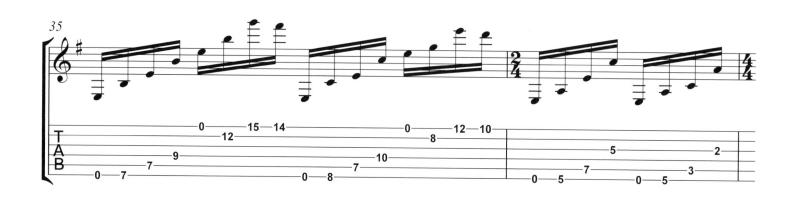

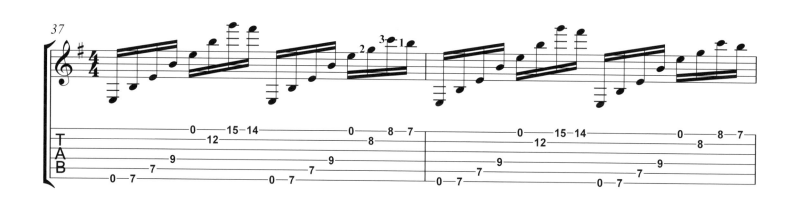

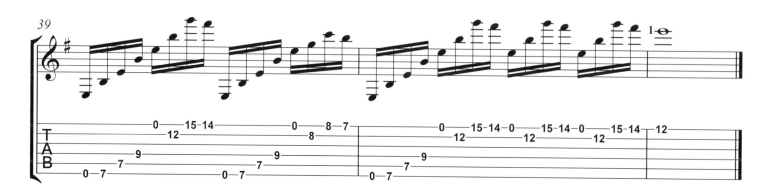

ETUDE IN A

Etude in A is one of the most interesting works, harmonically. It doesn't actually use the A major scale, but primarily uses a scale known as the *Aeolian Dominant* mode (for now, don't worry about what the term mode means – just think of the word 'mode' as a substitute for the word scale). To your ear, the A Aeolian Dominant mode will possibly sound 'Eastern' – maybe slightly Spanish/Arabic?

The work also plays with the idea of alternating major/minor: the initial phrase – which is major (the Aeolian Dominant mode is a form of a major scale) - is reiterated in bar 3, but using the minor scale. The change is relatively subtle to the ear, but effective. We can find other examples of major/minor shifting in bars 33 and 34, and bars 46 and 47.

Bar 17 is interesting: the second half of the bar is an *Augmented* arpeggio (the progression in bar 17 = F – Faug): if you're interested in jazz, it's probably worth memorising this augmented arpeggio sequence, as it could prove very useful (in jazz music you'll find lots of augmented chords).

Tip – augmented chords are great chords for adding tension to your compositions.

Rhythmic Groupings

Thinking in terms of standard 4/4 time is perfectly adequate for this etude (i.e. thinking of the semiquaver groupings as 4-4-4-4). However, feel free to subdivide the groupings in the manner that is most comfortable for you (in the first page I'm thinking of the semiquaver groupings as 6-5-5).

In bar 51 we change to 6/16: this isn't as scary as it sounds – just think 6-note groupings. The final bar changes back to 4/4 – feel free to hold the note for as long as you wish (i.e. longer than indicated). Slowing down toward the final note could possibly work well?

Suggested Minimum Tempo – 4 notes per beat @ 76BPM

ETUDE IN A

MUSIC BY KRIS LENNOX

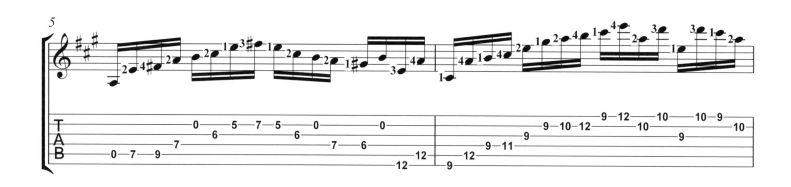

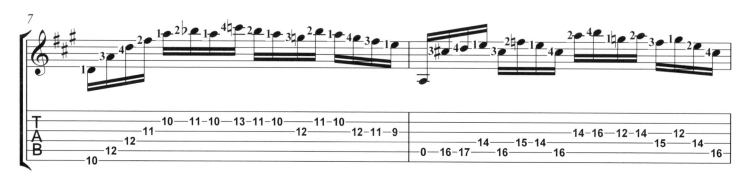

© Copyright 2015 Chester Music Limited.
All Rights Reserved. International Copyright Secured.

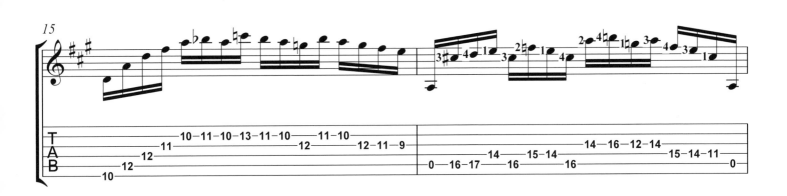

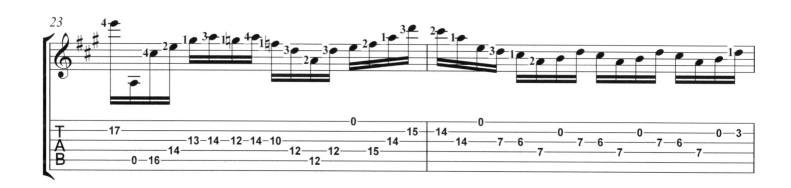

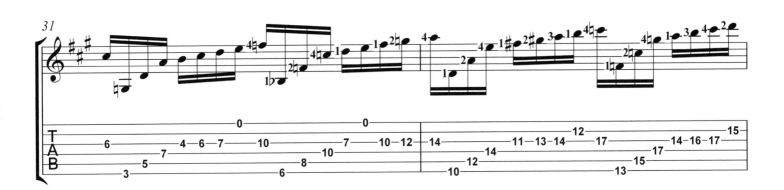

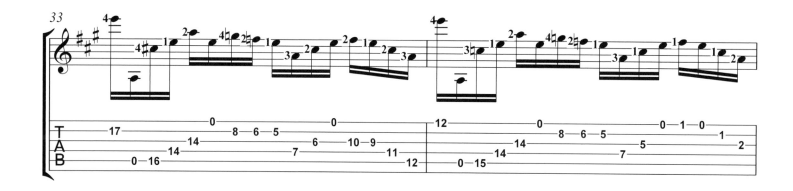

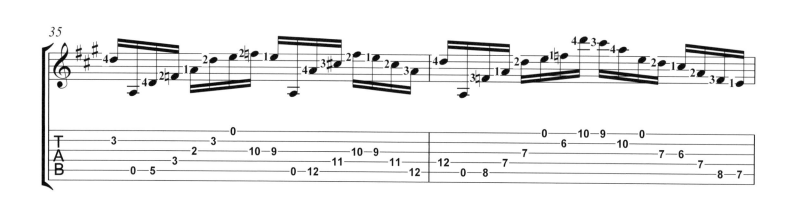

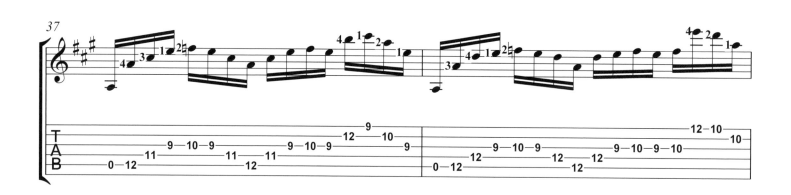

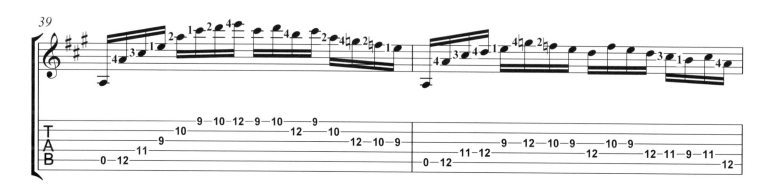

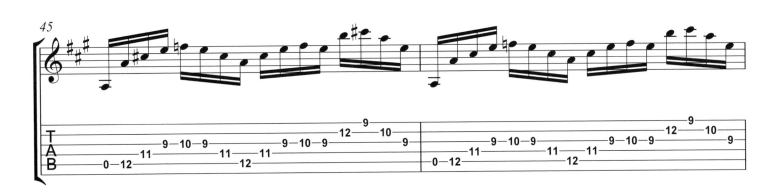

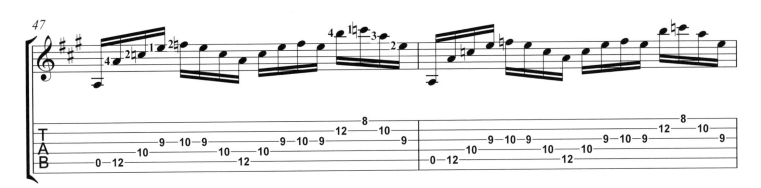

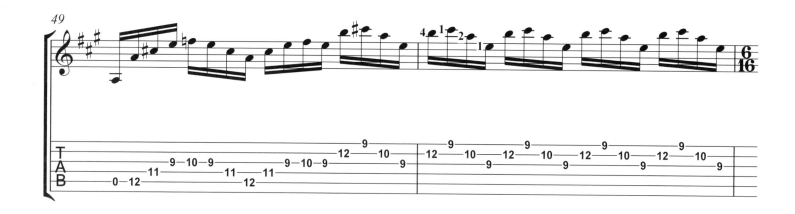

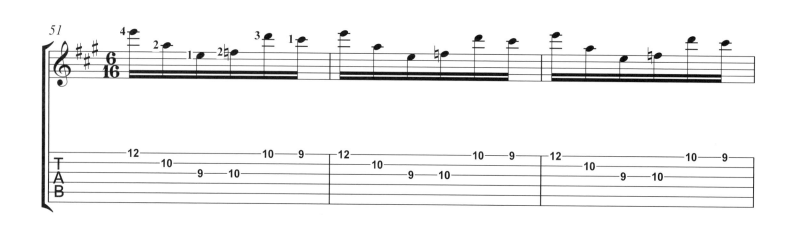

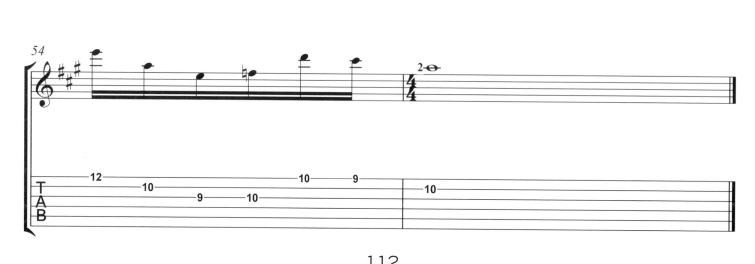

ETUDE IN Dm

Etude in Dm is an interesting piece in drop D tuning. The added depth of the 6th string tuned to D is capitalised on throughout the work, with most of the sequences rooted on the open 6th string.

The phrasing of this work should make it one of the easiest to learn (in terms of memory/note recall), with interesting short motifs (i.e. the first few bars), to the full 12-note *rolling arpeggios* (rolling arpeggio = going up and down through an arpeggio shape/sequence) of bars 31/32.

Some of the bars are 'stretchy' (i.e. bars 13/14); keep the wrist straight!

Etude in Dm is the only work featuring a chord (bar 47); this low open D5 chord brings the work - and the set – to a convincing conclusion.

Tip – drop tuning can add great depth to your compositions, but overuse can render drop tuning obsolete. Tasteful and selective use of drop tuning can be more effective than continual use of drop tuning.

Rhythmic Groupings

Bars 1-12: 6-6

Bars 13-16: 3-3-3-3

Bars 17-22: 6-6

Bar 23: 4-4-4

Bars 24-27: 6-6-6

Bar 28: 4-4-4

Bar 29: 4-5-3

Bar 30: 3-5-4

Bar 31-end: 6-6

Suggested Minimum Tempo – 2 notes per beat @ 178BPM

ETUDE IN Dm

MUSIC BY KRIS LENNOX

⑥ = D

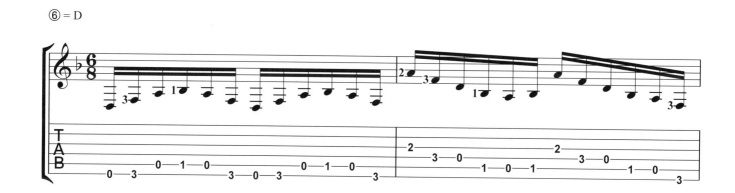

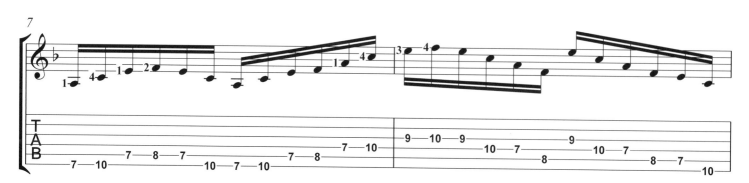

© Copyright 2015 Chester Music Limited.
All Rights Reserved. International Copyright Secured.

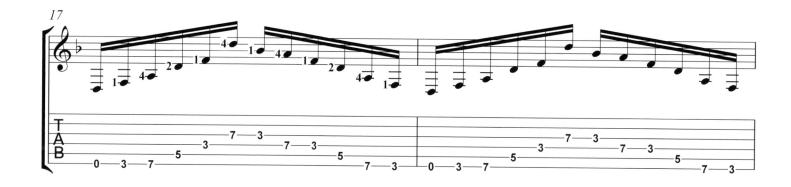

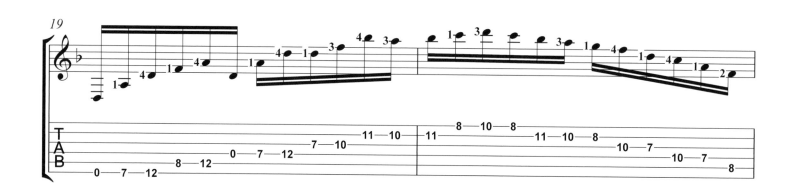

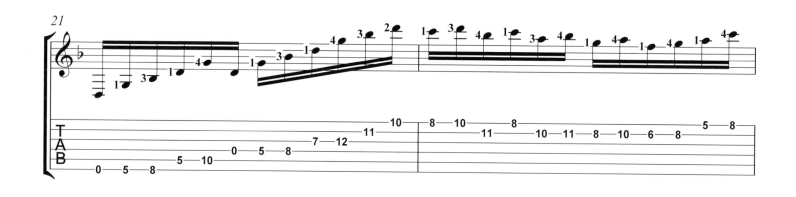

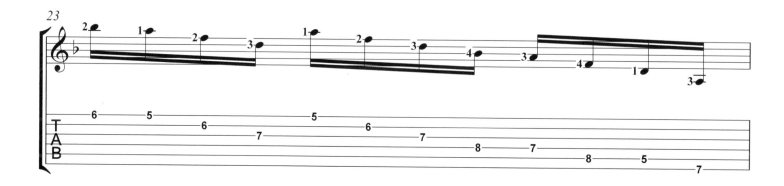

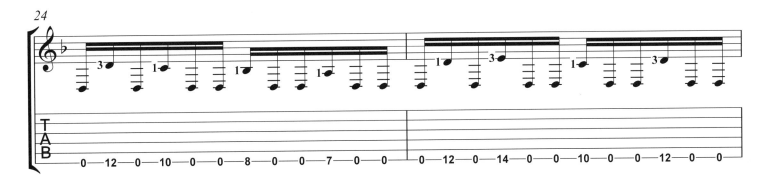

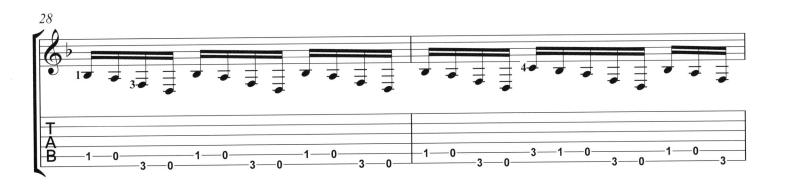

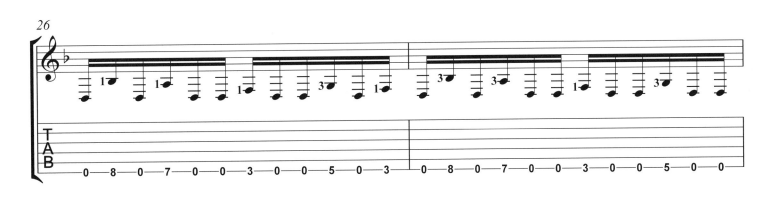

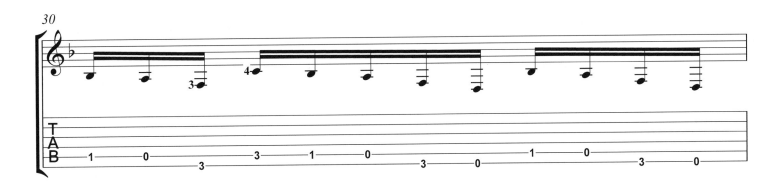

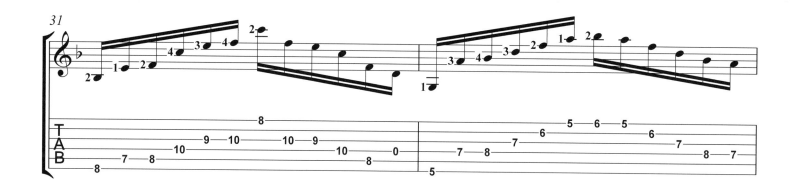

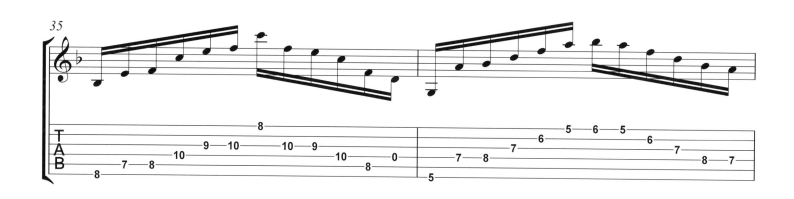

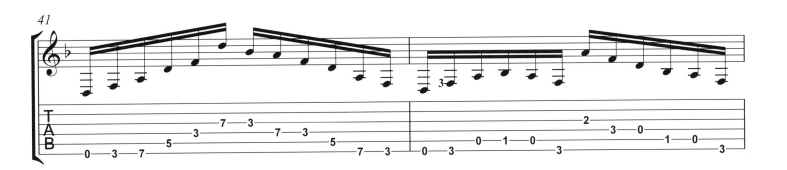

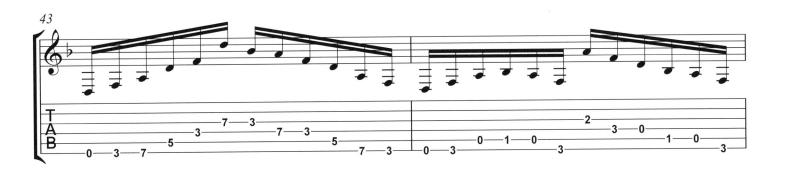

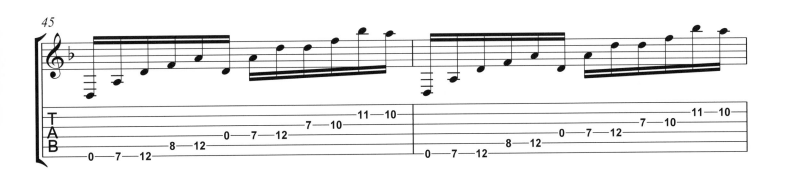

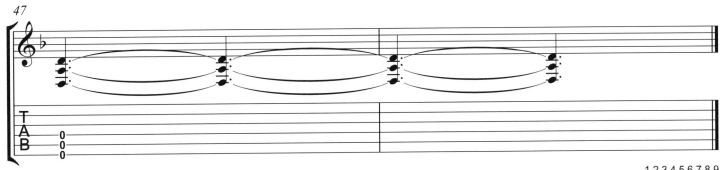

1 2 3 4 5 6 7 8 9

119

HOW TO DOWNLOAD YOUR MUSIC TRACKS

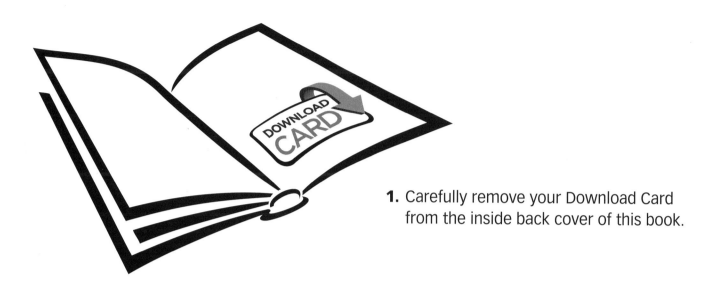

1. Carefully remove your Download Card from the inside back cover of this book.

TO REDEEM THIS CARD VISIT
www.musicsalesdownloads.com

ENTER ACCESS CODE:

XXXXXXXXX

Download Cards are powered by Dropcards.
User must accept terms at dropcards.com/terms
which are adopted by The Music Sales Group.
Not redeemable for cash. Void where prohibited or restricted by law.

DCARD1006478

2. On the back of the card is your unique access code. Enter this at www.musicsalesdownloads.com

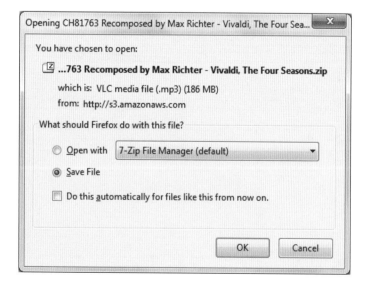

Opening CH81763 Recomposed by Max Richter - Vivaldi, The Four Sea...

You have chosen to open:

☑ ...763 Recomposed by Max Richter - Vivaldi, The Four Seasons.zip

which is: VLC media file (.mp3) (186 MB)
from: http://s3.amazonaws.com

What should Firefox do with this file?

○ Open with   7-Zip File Manager (default) ▾
◉ Save File

☐ Do this automatically for files like this from now on.

OK   Cancel

3. Follow the instructions to save your files to your computer*. That's it!

*Appearance of download manager will vary depending upon operating system and web browser.
In case of difficulty when downloading files, please contact dropcards.com/help
Card missing? Please contact music@musicsales.co.uk